Strategic Corporate Responsibility
The Social Dimension of Firms

Ulpiana Kocollari

Strategic Corporate Responsibility
The Social Dimension of Firms

First published 2018 by Routledge

2 Park Square, Milton Park, Abingdon, Oxfordshire OX14 4RN
52 Vanderbilt Avenue, New York, NY 10017

Routledge is an imprint of the Taylor & Francis Group, an informa business

First issued in paperback 2020

British Library Cataloguing-in-Publication Data
A catalogue record for this book is available from the British Library

ISBN: 978-88-921-1424-1 (hbk-G. Giappichelli Editore)
ISBN: 978-1-138-31342-2 (hbk-Routledge)
ISBN: 978-0-367-59051-2 (pbk-Routledge)

Typeset in Simoncini Garamond
by G. Giappichelli Editore, Turin, Italy

The manuscript has been subjected to the double blind peer review process prior to publication.

CONTENTS

page

LIST OF FIGURES AND TABLES

Figures

Tables

ACKNOWLEDGMENTS

I feel deeply indebted to the many people who supported me during my study and work on this project. I am extremely grateful to wise colleagues and advisors that guided me in this learning journey. I very much appreciate the engaging and encouraging discussions with Bernardo, Maddalena, Silvia and Stefano. I thank my generous friends for their constant presence and their support, most especially Niccolò P. A special thank you to **ANK Architecture** for the 3D graphics.

INTRODUCTION

"Business is a vital partner in achieving the Sustainable Development Goals.
Companies can contribute through their core activities,
and we ask companies everywhere to assess their impact,
set ambitious goals and communicate transparently about the results."

Ban Ki-moon, United Nations Secretary-General [1]

This study aims to move the debate on Corporate Social Responsibility and Sustainability forward by focusing on the opportunities and synergies that these issues can represent for the innovation of business processes and for redefining the competitiveness of firms operating in a fast-changing environment.

The increasing concentration on and regulation of the social and environmental externalities caused by firms' activities have raised awareness of strategy, management structure, performance and impact measurements, workforce, and culture – issues that draw attention to stakeholder-oriented management models. For both firms and stakeholders, the importance of understanding and measuring the social and environmental impact of business activities has grown rapidly, and has deeply influenced the entire economic and productive ecosystem.

In order to address these issues, firms' activities are analysed through the patterns made up of the relationships between stakeholders, the resources they bring to the firm and their expected rewards from its activities. This approach allows the identification of dynamic management tools that consider both the firm's social and economic dimensions simultaneously.

The aim of this work is to understand: *"How the configuration of a firm's social dimension can help identify inclusive corporate governance models, define innovative management processes and re-shape performance measurement systems for the evaluation and assessment of sustainable economic, social and environmental results"*.

---

[1] GRI, U. WBSCD, SDG compass, *The guide for business action on the SDGs*, SDG Compass, 2015, p. 4, retrieved at https://sdgcompass.org/wp-content/uploads/2015/12/01 9104_SDG_Compass_Guide_2015.pdf.

The proposed conceptual framework goes beyond the trade-offs between firms' social and economic performance, highlighting the strategic role of their social dimension, and suggests a positive relationship between sustainability-orientation and the likelihood of efficient and innovative management processes guided by stakeholder accountability principles.

The setting-up of appropriate corporate governance models, management processes, and measurement and reporting tools for socially oriented business activities can contribute to firms' innovation processes and profitable growth while addressing stakeholders' social and environmental needs. The proposed framework is analysed in the cases of two different types of firms, operating in two diverse business stages – Innovative Startups with a Social Goal and Benefit Corporations – representing two different configurations of the social dimension and two distinct stages of the evolution of firms' socially oriented activities.

The work is organized as follows.

The first chapter aims to study the importance of the firm's social dimension and how it is configured in the firm's exchanges within its overall system, consisting of the market system and the other rules and institutions that constitute its operative and competitive landscape. The firm's relationship with its environment is embodied in its more or less formally defined interactions with its different interest groups – stakeholders. Stakeholder theory, based on this concept, offers an alternative way of looking at the company, modifying its governance borders and the role of intangible resources such as culture and values in management processes. In view of need to emphasize this complexity, originating from the large number of parties concerned and the variety of resources involved in firms' activities, the necessity arises to include both economic and social dimensions when tracing the patterns embedded in the firm's exchanges within its overall system, which can influence its management choices.

By applying the proposed perspective – integrating social and economic dimensions in firms' management framework, it is possible not only to identify the "actors" (shareholders, stakeholders, communities, etc.) in corporate governance, but also to consider their links to various contributions (both tangible and intangible) and their multiple expectations on firm's performance (social and economic rewards). Accurate identification of these patterns of parties – contributions – rewards, and the analysis of their evolution within the firm's overall system can help managers to pinpoint appropriate inclusive governance models and at the same time to establish the right paths for the management processes and instruments that consider simultaneously the two dimensions.

After reviewing the current state of the art of Corporate Social Responsibility (CSR) studies, the second chapter proposes a framework giving due consideration to social dimension patterns in order to allow companies to assess their business in terms of social and environmental performance on a company– and project-specific level. This framework could facilitate the further implementation of socially oriented activities and performance and support effective decision-making processes. Particular attention is paid to its application in the context of firms' innovation and crisis management.

Even though various studies have investigated the relationship between a firm's social and economic performances, the progress of research into the field of stakeholder management and CSR today indicates that it is difficult to figure out the extent of firms' effective contribution to the resolution of social and environmental needs and how and how much this affects their economic results. Many firms are aware that social and environmental issues are important to business, but they still consider them to be at the periphery of companies' management and decision-making. If social and environmental issues were treated as "internalities" instead of externalities, they would no longer be considered as criticalities bringing trade-offs for firms' management, but as a means of transitioning to a different overall state – potentially the source of opportunities for improving firms' effectiveness and innovation.

The purpose of the management framework proposed, which considers both economic and social spheres, is to challenge this dualism by providing a two-way model that interprets the firm's activities and performance and provides a management platform for emerging adaptive social and economic party – contribution – reward patterns. The focus on the patterns can help firms to coherently manage a flow of issues (both economic and social) rather than dealing with the parties separately, losing sight of the interaction among them. The adoption of appropriate integrative mechanisms that link the two dimensions can affect firm's value creation process.

The framework also provides an explanation of how the synergies between the patterns of the firm's social and economic dimensions can mediate the management of many activities considered as externalities, which can be crucial in shaping firm's response to innovation and to a variety of criticalities.

The third chapter aims to analyse the role of social dimension measurement in the firm's management, given that the choice of social and environmental impact measurement model plays an important role in stakeholder accountability on the one hand, and on the other may influence the company's social accounting process for the assessment and reporting of its social performance.

The demand for new methods for measuring social impact has come from many different players, who wish to demonstrate the impact of their business activities for their stakeholders and the environment. Therefore, during the last few decades there has been a multiplication of measurement systems for satisfying the most widely varying demands for information about the social impact generated by firms, giving rise to many calculation methods.

Considering the needs and main characteristics of stakeholder accountability, this chapter proposes a four step process for social accounting and uses it as the basis for analysing the most widely quoted measurement models and their main features at a conceptual and operating level.

The four steps accounting process proposed starts by identifying the categories of data to be gathered, prioritized and processed in order to subsequently measure social and environmental benefits and costs, for evaluation of a firm's performance in both the social and the economic dimensions. In the two final steps, reporting, consideration is given to the choice of the instruments to be used to "translate" and disseminate information to the company's stakeholders both internally and externally, to allow in a final step the implementation of the data in the decision-making process.

The social and environmental impact measurement model should be chosen as appropriate to the steps in this process and the peculiarities and dynamics of the main characteristics of the firm's social dimension and its synergies with the economic dimension. The scale of the measurement process and its main purposes therefore need to be analysed in greater depth in relation to the varying information needs of the different patterns within the social and economic dimensions. Directive 2014/95/EU has fostered this process and further encouraged the adoption of suitable instruments for stakeholder accountability and for improving the disclosure of non-financial information, since it requires large companies to disclose specific information about the way they operate and how they manage social and environmental challenges.

Finally, the last chapter analyses the application of the proposed social dimension framework in the case of two distinct types of firms – Innovative Startups with a Social Goal and Benefit Corporations – by making a more detailed assessment of the opportunities it offers for firm's management and decision-making and its limits from an operative perspective. The two cases are chosen in order to capture different configurations of the patterns of the firm's social dimension, as in the case of Social Goal Startups the social dimension is intrinsic to the entrepreneurship project, while in Benefit Corporations it can be added to the core set of traditional economic processes. Furthermore, these two types of firms, operating in two different stages of the business life cycle, are able to exemplify different performance management issues and diverse measurement and communication needs. The assessment of social and environmental impact and its disclosure, the direct consequence of the selection of adequate measurement models, requires the correct configuration of the patterns of both social and economic dimensions. The various parties – contributions – rewards pattern configurations, identified through the interactive exchange between the economic and social dimensions in these firms, generate different requirements for the social accounting process. However, in both forms of organization, the measurement model entails a greater involvement of all stakeholders in the accounting process, in order to evaluate the relevance of the issues and the data reported.

The analysis of social performance measurement in each of the two categories of firms investigated highlights not only the tailoring of the measurement model to the characteristics of the social dimension, but also the need for a personalized process of its adoptions, with the aim of achieving integrated managerial control and communication for both social and economic performance.

Chapter 1
THE SOCIAL DIMENSION OF FIRMS

1.1. The firm's overall system

The firm, viewed as an evolving system, relates and interacts with the market system and other rules and institutions named "environmental systems", which constitute a set of conditions and circumstances within which the firm is located and can be defined as the firm's overall system. In traditional business studies, this system of conditions and circumstances, whatever their origin and type, in which the firm finds the conditions for its survival and development, represents the general environment in which it operates[1]. Given the complexity and variety of the relationships between the firm and its environment, we can differentiate between the general and the specific environment. Within the general environment, its interconnected characteristics can be classified on the basis of their degree of interdependence. This categorization helps us identify the specific systems that make up the general environment. Consequently, the general environment can be subdivided into the following systems[2]:

• physical-natural environment;
• political and institutional enviroment;
• economic environment;
• social-cultural environment.

In order to define each of the four systems that build up the firm's overall system, and thus the effects that they may have on firms' activities and how they relate to the specific environment, the sections which follow will attempt to identify the variables that characterize each of these subgroups.

---

[1] Ferrero G., *Impresa e management*, Giuffrè, Milano, 1987.
[2] Similar classifications are proposed in Ferrero 1987, Bruni 1990 and Bertini 1990.

Figure 1. Firm's overall system.

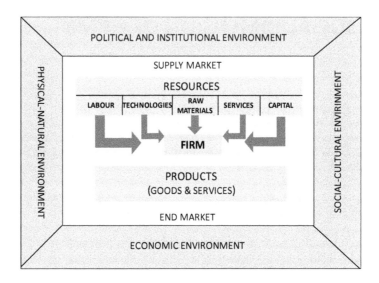

Source: Elaboration of the model proposed in Ferrero, 1987.

The physical-natural environment includes environmental constraints composed of geographic and demographic variables that characterize the context in which the company carries out its business[3]. This type of environment may impose constraints regarding environmental protection or the lack or scarcity of natural resources, but it can also provide opportunities through the use of accessible resources, the creation of substitutes for natural resources or their conservation and regeneration, the formation and development of markets, technologies and products capable of exploiting natural resources and limiting environmental pollution; etc.[4].

The political and institutional environment comprises the legal framework, the political regime and the institutions of the state or states in which firms operate. The variables that characterize this type of environment interact strongly with those of the specific environment and more directly with the firm's economic patterns.

The organization of the general economic system determines how markets function by influencing their demand structure and by establishing

---

[3] Ranalli F., *Il sistema aziendale: aspetti costitutivi ed evolutivi*, in Cavalieri E., Ranalli F., *Economia Aziendale vol. II. Aree funzionali e governo aziendale*, Giappichelli, Torino, 1999.

[4] The relationship between the firm and natural environment is covered in Miolo Vitali P. 1978, Catturi G. 1990.

policies and tools for monitoring operations and operators' behaviours. All these conditions have a massive influence on the way in which the business system operates in these markets. Nevertheless, we must not forget the ambivalence of this relationship, as, by its modus operandi, the firm also affects the structural characteristics of the various markets and their functioning. In this way, firms themselves may influence and change the patterns of the economic environment.

The social and cultural environments are made up of interrelated variables, which is why they are ordered together. The structure of society in the places where the company operates, with its stratification in classes of subjects aggregated in homogeneous groups, and their degree of mobility, is particularly important. The cultural environment is characterized by the creation and dissemination of knowledge, values and ideologies in the social context in which the firm develops.

A similar definition of the general environment is also found in North American literature with particular reference to the general context in which the firm operates. This approach subdivides the general environment where the firm operates into four main segments: social, economic, political and technological[5]. The only difference between the two conceptualizations lies in the presence of a different category – the technological segment, which includes the new products, processes, and materials deriving from technological innovation and the state of advancement of knowledge in science, in theoretical and operational terms.

Moving on to the specific environment, attention shifts to the components of the external environment with which the firm interacts most directly. Indeed, the specific environment is often taken to be synonymous with the markets in which the company is a player through its processes of exchange and supply of resources and/or to through the sale of its products or services, and can be identified as comprising the labour market, raw materials market, capital market, service market, technology market and end market. Another way of sorting the variables that compose the specific environment to allow investigation of the main issues in the relationships between the firm and the specific environment is to identify those that are part of the firm's competitive landscape[6]. In this additional group, the competitive environment is further subdivided into the business areas within which competition between companies takes place, as described in Porter's model of actors and competitive forces[7].

---

[5] Fahey L., Narayanan V.K., *Macroenvironmental analysis for strategic management*, St. Paul: West, 1986, pp. 28-30.

[6] Coda V., *L'orientamento strategico dell'impresa*, Utet, Torino, 1988, pp. 13-14.

[7] Porter M.E., *Il vantaggio competitivo*, Edizioni di comunità, Milano, 1987, pp. 10-15.

The firm's development is therefore dependent on its ability to align it-self with the dynamics of the overall system to which it belongs and to the demands and changes of which it must pay constant attention[8]. In the light of these considerations, the firm could be seen as an organism composed of a multiplicity of relationships that reach across its different dimensions: spatial, temporal, social, economic, institutional, etc. It can be defined as a "complex machine" in which all its dimensions, in turn, are complex drivers that interact with each other in multiple combinations. This purely conceptual "machine" is also an unpredictable model, since a given input will not necessarily always provide the same output[9]. The variety of the final state, and therefore of the outputs, is due to the multiplicity of the internal and external factors. Its complexity is also linked to the uniqueness of the individuals who established and are part of the firm. Each of them acts differently in response to their own individual evaluation systems, increasing the degree of complexity of the entire system, which therefore does not have a definite limit on its number of patterns, since it does not have a pre-established number of behaviours.

1.2. Grounding relationships within the firm's overall system: Stakeholder Theory

The firm's relationship with its environments takes the form of interactions with its different interest groups, which are more or less formally defined. Some of these groupings consist of categories of individuals, while others may be organizations and various institutions. Each of these groups, organizations, and institutions is a body of people linked together by a common cause or a shared view on a specific issue related to the firm's activities[10]. Thus, a firm's relational activities, within its overall system, are defined as its cooperation with the various actors, the level of communication among the various parties and the ways in which the company itself comes into contact with its surrounding environments. The nodes in these relational networks are the different individuals or groups that, depending on their different expectations, think, communicate and use multiple perspectives for the exchange of information and therefore introduce a certain amount of "noise" and complexity into the overall system. This may take the form

---

[8] Chirieleison C., *Le strategie sociali nel governo dell'azienda*, Giuffrè, Milano, 2002.

[9] Bocchi G., Ceruti M., *La sfida della complessità*, Mondadori, Milano, 2007, pp. 155-169.

[10] Carroll A.B., Buchholtz A.K., *Business and society. Ethics and stakeholder management*, South-Western, Div. of Thomson Learning, New York, 2005.

of criticism of the firm, but even this can be transformed into a resource, offering multiple opportunities, if it is used as input for identifying alternative solutions to problems in the overall system that can then be converted into benefits for the business.

The groups of people who may influence or who in turn are influenced by the firm's business are known as "stakeholders" in the management literature. Stakeholder theory, which is based on this concept, offers an alternative way of looking at the company, no longer restricted only to employees, suppliers, and consumers, organized for the pursuit of the interest of a single group of stakeholders: equity investors (shareholders). Scholars focusing on stakeholder theory criticize the traditional model of the company and its excessive emphasis on shareholders, because it fails to take into account other stakeholders, who may be equally important for the pursuance of the company's mission. According to these studies, other stakeholder groups may have just as much influence on the business as shareholders, and therefore firms' objectives must go beyond the satisfaction of shareholders' interests by also including the needs and demands of the other stakeholders in their management processes.

Freeman is generally considered to have originated stakeholder theory in his "Strategic Management: a stakeholder approach" (1984), but in reality, the concept that this term expresses and its relationship to the corporate system can be found in many previous studies. In the international literature, the origins of the general idea expressed by stakeholder theory can be traced to notions developed with reference to corporate social responsibility, and other issues related to business management, system theory, and organizational theory. The roots of the social dimension of the firm can be clearly identified in early studies of management.

Corporate responsibility studies acknowledge the company's obligations, and view the company as a set of groups of stakeholders, of whom shareholders are only one. These studies clearly state the concept which is also the basis of stakeholder theory, without however coining the term stakeholder. Berle and Means (1932) in one of their last studies of the separation of ownership and control, invoke the concept represented by the term stakeholder in stating that: "... the control groups have, rather, cleared the way for the claims of a group far wider than either the owner or the control. They have placed the community in a position to demand that modern corporations serve not just their owners or the controllers but all society ..."[11].

---

[11] Berle A., Means G., *Private property and the modern corporation*, Comerce Clearing House, New York, 1932, p. 312.

Another early perspective, which considers the role of stakeholders as fundamental through another approach, is set out in management planning and control studies. As Freeman (1984) himself observes, the term stakeholder was used for the first time in the Standards Research Institute in 1963 to define those groups without the support of which the firm would cease to exist. In this vision, the planning process could not be implemented without understanding the interests of different stakeholder groups. The fundamental difference represented by this vision compared to that proposed by the stakeholder theory is that the former limits the concept of stakeholders only to those central to the very survival of the firm.

Other important pre-stakeholder concepts are proposed in organizational studies [12], where the most significant in terms of equivalence with the current stakeholder theory is the work of Pfeffer and Salancik (1978). In their conceptualization, the importance of the resources needed to conduct the business is accentuated by the firm's dependence on providers of resources and support. Although these studies describe mutual interdependence in the relations between the company and its stakeholders, they do not recognize their mutual value, generated by the company's role as a reward provider for its stakeholders.

Other initial notions and initial developments of some of the concepts of stakeholder theory can be found in the theory of complex systems. According to this view, many social phenomena cannot be analysed individually but should be considered as part of a larger system, where they interact with other elements. Under this principle, the role assigned to stakeholders in the overall system is a more active one, since the optimization of the system's individual objectives is only pursued if compatible with the pursuit of its global objectives [13].

Given the multiplicity of the studies and concepts related to the term stakeholder, in order to contextualize Stakeholder Theory in the management literature, we will attempt to return to its lines of evolution and its main shared concepts in the academic field. Here, the categorization of topics related to this issue, proposed by Donaldson and Preston (1995), can offer useful guidance. The study identifies four main features of stakeholder theory, which contribute to the process by which it was acclaimed as a theory, differentiating it from a simple set of ideas related to the concept of stakeholder. According to the central thesis proposed in the study,

---

[12] Emery F., Trist E., *The casual texture of organizational environments,* Human relations, 1966, 18, pp. 21-31; Pfeffer J., Salancik G., *The external control of organization*, Harper, New York, 1978.

[13] Ackoff R., *Redesigning the future,* John Wiley, New York, 1974.

stakeholder theory is descriptive, instrumental, normative, and manageri- al[14]. It is descriptive, as the scholars who illustrate it report descriptive models for the firm. The configuration they propose is a constellation of simultaneously cooperative and competing interests, with intrinsic values embedded in them. Another distinctive feature of stakeholder theory is that it is instrumental in the type of correlation analysed between stakeholder management activities and the corresponding results in terms of the firm's performance. This property occurs in studies which aim to verify hypothe- ses such as: if stakeholder management principles are taken into considera- tion, then given the other conditions, the company will have positive results in terms of economic performance (profitability, growth, etc.).

Although the first two features are fundamental to stakeholder theory, Donaldson and Preston recognize the normative component as the funda- mental element that provides the "glue" for all the other elements. Norma- tive aspects provide descriptive behavioural principles that can help in evaluating managerial choices.

The last thesis argues that stakeholder theory is a managerial theory in the broad sense of the term. It does not only describe existing situations or predict cause-effect relationships, but suggests attitudes, structures, and practices that, if taken together, can constitute stakeholder management. Under this thesis, stakeholder management aims to identify organizational structures, general policies, and individual decisions, the main characteristic of which is a simulta- neous attention to the legitimate interests of all the firm's stakeholders[15].

The work of Donaldson and Preston helps to clarify the main character- istics of stakeholder theory, useful for bringing together its main elements, identified in the various disciplines. Their analysis makes it possible to cat- egorize individual contributions in terms of a few main strands, and thus build up a common skeleton from all the previous studies, to serve as guide for the future development of this theory. But despite its widely acknowl- edged usefulness, there are several grounds for criticism of this approach. Firstly, it does not provide criteria for identifying the company's stakehold- ers and evaluating their "stake" in the company. Secondly, if we look care- fully at what the study states and the idea that it transmits, stakeholder the- ory can be seen as an alternative theory to the shareholder profit-oriented model. This distinction can lead to a contrast between the two models, to the point of considering them as two totally different and irreconcilable ways of thinking and of analysing businesses' prerogatives.

---

[14] Donaldson T., Preston L., *La teoria degli stakeholder dell'impresa: concetti, evi- denza ed implicazioni*, in Freeman E.R., Rusconi G., Dorigatti M., *Teoria degli stake- holder*, Franco Angeli, Milano, 2007.

[15] *Ibidem.*

Considering these issues, Freeman (2002) did not identify stakeholder theory as a specific theory in his later work, but associated it with all the other research strands, in which every goal the firm pursues can identify a set of responsibilities for managers as they implement these goals [16]. According to this further development, the "shareholder approach" is in turn part of the "stakeholder approach".

Although these studies express on the one hand the singularity of this theory, and on the other, its generality, they both converge in a common tendency to recognize the normative component of stakeholders' interests as central to any study of the firm. Indeed, both the opposing studies identify the distinctive feature of stakeholder theory in just this normative approach. This position can be useful for assessing whether a given company is responding satisfactorily to the requirements imposed by its mission and its managers' obligations to its stakeholders.

From this brief review, we have seen that although it is relatively recent, stakeholder theory has a rich past and a promising future, aimed at resolving many divergences arising from the numerous studies that apply this approach for the investigation of many different areas in various business disciplines. However, the fundamental reflection that this theory offers, for the purposes of the analysis of the firm's social dimension, is the question that it puts with regard to the firm's new tasks. Moreover, the question of defining the firm's management prerogatives becomes a central factor that management studies, in particular, must take into account. As well as supplying goods and services to satisfy customers' needs, the firm must also come up with ways of meeting the expectations of the various stakeholders who control the resources it requires for its business.

If the firm's goal is to maximize value for its stakeholders, this means adopting an appropriate decision-making system, which refers to the firm viewed as a community of interests made up of different categories of stakeholders and the multiple relationships among them. This view may represent a particular case of Network Theory, where the different categories of interests are organized into formally defined groups connected with each other, as in the relationships between firms [17].

If stakeholder theory is applied to the firm's overall system, several categories of relationships fundamental to the normal implementation of business activities emerge. At an initial level, these include the relationships between the various productive factors: in-depth knowledge of their peculiar-

---

[16] Jones T.M., Wicks A.C., Freeman E.R., *Stakeholder theory: the state of art*, in Bowie N.E., *The Blackwell guide to business ethics*, Blackwell Publisher, 2002, pp. 9-35.

[17] Cattaneo M., *Principi di valutazione del capitale d'impresa*, Il Mulino, Bologna, 1998, pp. 16-32.

ities and their relevance to the production process can bring advantages in terms of efficiency. At a second level, there is the relationship among the different categories of stakeholders, fundamental for coordination processes and for meeting their expectations regarding the achievement of monetary and non-monetary rewards. The existence of these relationships on the one hand helps stakeholders to act collectively and on the other increases the spread of trust and information on firms' long-term prospects. Finally, the third level consists of relationships between companies, typically between companies carrying out different activities within the value chain, or between companies belonging to the same industrial districts, both based on the recognition of values such as trust and reciprocity.

Given the importance of the system of relationships and its various implications in the configuration of the firm's social dimension, it must also be considered during the design and construction of the management infrastructure and the mechanisms for evaluating its performance.

1.3. Definition and coordinates of the firm's social dimension

The decision to include both economic and social dimensions when tracing the patterns embedded in the firm's exchanges within in its overall system arises from the need to emphasize the complexity originating from the large number of parties concerned and the variety of resources involved in the exchanges between the firm and its environments. Two further variables, space and time, also need to be added to this complex picture, as they are essential for studying the modern firm, which operates in a long-term perspective and is at the centre of the phenomenon of globalization. The complexity of the physical, relational and regulatory factors, as well as the economic ones, which characterize a firm's activities in its various environments, makes the conceptualization of its social dimension a dynamic and complex undertaking.

The social dimension is designed as part of the firm, adding new values to it and marking out new lines for its evolution, while at the same time, the firm itself and its new infrastructures become fundamental for the social dimension, modifying its borders and creating substantial changes in their turn.

Even the systemic view of the firm does not represent it as a set of autonomous elements, but views it as an economic complex, determined not only by its individual constituent parts, but also by the relations that arise between them in the dynamic context of the general coordination of business activities.

In order to capture and measure the current value of the patterns and the gap between their actual state and the opportunities for their evolution currently available within the firm's overall system, both time and space coordinates should be considered. They are both parts of and bridges between the firm's social and economic dimensions viewed within a given time horizon. Therefore, a firm can be analysed by means of the dynamics of the relationships between individuals or groups of individuals, their exchanges and expectations ordered within the patterns of each subsystem identified within a given overall system.

We have seen how the two entities – the firm and its overall system – are closely interrelated, through what can be viewed as a structure of relationships that form an indispensable, unbroken link from the macro level of the time-space of the whole context of the business's world to the micro-context, consisting of the system of relationships in which the single firm interacts. Studied within this context, the firm's activities are represented as the patterns visible to a specific observer analysing a firm located in a certain space at a given moment. Within this configuration, thanks to the development of communication systems, the events and processes which co-exist across physical space can be managed jointly thanks to the ability to handle Big Data and the speed with which large amounts of information can be transferred. Physical space consists of locations that each have their own identity and history, re-creating a representation of a multiplicity of relationships rooted in an experienced time. One example is the geographic proximity space which provides the symbolic reference for a community's identity, while simultaneously being shaped by the community itself [18].

It is thus possible to build a "neural" space in which the firm's activity (the heart of the overall system) is located, parallel with the physical space in which we are traditionally used to locating a production activity. A place made up of patterns of discontinuous but interconnected points, of simultaneous communications and reactions, and not necessarily sequential timelines, which are all part of an entity of a higher order [19].

In addition, according to business administration studies, a firm must operate in compliance with economic principles, in order to pursue the economic equilibrium that will enable it to survive over time in a changing environment [20]. Space and time are simultaneously both the invariants related to the time elapsed and the variables of a future time for the relational complex between the firm and its environments. These variables strongly

---

[18] Mandich G., *Spazio tempo. Prospettive sociologiche*, Franco Angeli, Milano, 1996.

[19] Agostinelli M., *Tempo e spazio nell'impresa postfordista*, Manifestolibri, Roma, 1997.

[20] Masini C., *Lavoro e risparmio*, Utet, Torino, 1979.

influence the economic equilibrium and suggest that it should really be viewed as a dynamic concept: i.e. the confirmation of the principles of economic sustainability over the long term. This creates a space-time context within which the firm's different patterns are configured as it evolves within the overall system. When investigating the firm's realm, the aggregated parties it involves, the activities it performs and the results it obtains must all be assigned on the basis of the coordinates dictated by the specified space/time values.

Figure 2. Graphic representation of the firm's social dimension and its determinants.

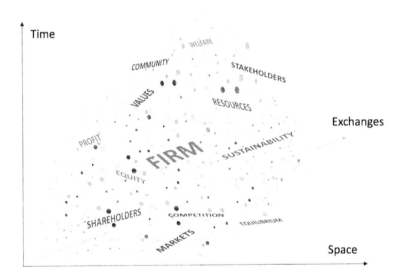

The potential determinants of the firm's social dimension are: the patterns established through exchanges with the specific environment, closest to the business activities that are most frequently replicated, and the general environment, in which exchanges cover a larger amount of the geographic space perspective but are less frequent (as represented in the diagram in Figure 1: the patterns of the specific environment are closer to the firm while those of the general environment are further away and more widely scattered); time, which may determine different configurations for the short and long term; and place, in the sense of the distance in geographic space between a specific location where the company was born and a location where it conducts its business, consisting of distances and other more complex context measurements. The diagram also shows a positive relationship between the space variable and the amplitude of the patterns.

In fact, with increasing geographical distances there is also an increase in the number of patterns, as new patterns can be identified during the transition towards the general environment.

The social dimension of firms is defined as the long-term projection of the configuration of the patterns embedded in the firm's exchanges within in its overall system.

1.4. The drivers of the firm's social dimension

Taking the coordinates of the firm's social dimension into account, the following paragraphs will set out to identify its main patterns, created by the different configurations of the interactions among its variables. The social perspective discussed in the business and management literature will be reviewed with the aim of analysing and investigating the firm's social dimension and its configurations.

As we have already seen, the overall system in which the firm operates is a complex one. We have moved from a framework where there was only one category of interests in relation to the firm – that of its owners, who had access to the resources needed to start the economic activity – to the present infrastructure, with a multiplicity of interest groups with resources and expectations bound up in the entrepreneurial activity. Since in the past the owner and the manager were often one and the same, it became necessary over time to identify another group of people that carried out the company's productive activities – the employees. After that, the owners needed suppliers of the raw materials required for production, and people to buy the goods or services they provided – customers. In short, we are now in the last stage of a long evolutionary process, the initial phases of which had a less "crowded" framework, with fewer expectations on the part of the various individuals and groups involved in the company.

Referring to a firm operating in today's society, in order to describe and understand how and why the framework has evolved from a simple to a complex configuration, we need to analyse the main forces driving the transformation of society itself. Even though this is not the subject and the scope of this work, within this process we can identify the main evolutionary factors associated with businesses and in particular identify the central role that the firm plays in this process. To identify the firm's organizational infrastructure and management model, it becomes crucial to understand its different constituencies, which can have a direct influence on its viability and survival (Hillman and Keim, 2001), and the strategic resources they bring to the firm and that represent their stake in it.

The modern firm is institutionally one of the mainstays of a "fast-moving" society comprising many groups that represent a multitude of interests, expectations, and demands, which a firm aims to satisfy through its business, undertaken to fulfil evolving social and economic needs. As it performs this role, it must manage the set of relationships with its vast number of not always clearly identifiable stakeholders. This phenomenon is directly represented in the firm's social dimension, and at the same time may further modify its composition and configuration. In order to obtain a dynamic, clear representation of the firm's social dimension, many key elements for its construction must be analysed in the evolutionary history of its main components.

1.4.1. Corporate governance

Moving on to the new vision of the firm provided by stakeholder theory, new perspectives emerge about the models for managing a large number of interest groups and pursuing the company's mission. We have seen that besides the goal of creating profit for shareholders, managers are called upon to manage a multitude of interests sustained by stakeholder groups, which affect the path followed by companies as they work towards their overall goals and in their operations. In an initial stage, they are required to identify the firm's different categories of stakeholders, defined by the subsystems with which the firm interacts, and the influence they have on its mission-driven activities. This process also detects the types of relationships that the company establishes with these groups, based on the collaborations needed to carry out the company's business activities. After identifying the firm's stakeholders and their expectations of the firm, a process of mutual exchange should be established, in which both parties draw on their perception and knowledge of each other to articulate their mutual expectations and future behaviours. An important distinction can be made on the basis of the type of expectations that are taken into account, and in particular their nature as defined by their degree of legitimacy. The main difference that can be made is between an interest that a party may have in the business activity and a right legally recognized by the signing of a contract. This process is required because the company's exchanges with its different stakeholders may present a range of risks if their expectations are not met, but it can also help to recognise the opportunities that they represent and which therefore need to be managed. Generating the consent of the firm's stakeholders who control the resources it requires, through a variety of formal arrangements, guarantees the firm the resources and any partnerships needed for the achievement of its goals and the conduct of its business.

In this new configuration, described above, the firm's relationships become broader and diverse and at the same time their influence on the design of its corporate governance and its management infrastructure increases.

If we consider the definition of corporate governance – "… the structure of rights and responsibilities among the parties with a stake in the firm …"[21], the individuals or groups of individuals that represent the parties and their interests – some of the main patterns that make up the firm's social dimension – may influence its corporate governance model. In fact, the organizational structure defines the configuration of the interest groups, the contributions that these individuals provide to the organization, the rewards and benefits they receive from it, the main aim of the institution, the institutional ends, and the governance structures which regulate the long-term dynamic equilibrium between the stakeholders, their contributions and the rewards they expect[22] (Figure 3). Referring to the firm's design within its overall system, corporate governance represents the ordered structure adopted by the firm to govern patterns in the social and economic realms.

Figure 3. *Parties – Contributions – Rewards* conceptual scheme.

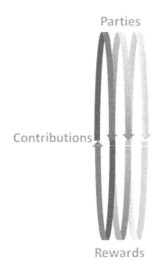

Source: Elaboration of the concept presented in Airoldi et al., 1995.

---

[21] Aok, M., *Information, corporate governance and institutional diversity: Competitiveness in Japan, the USA, and the transitional economies*, Oxford University Press, Inc, 2000, p. 11.

[22] Airoldi G., Amatori F., Invernizzi G., *Proprietà e Governo delle Aziende Italiane*, Egea, Milano, 1995.

The model of corporate governance firms adopt has become important not only for their internal organization but also for all the other organizations connected to their activities. Many studies in the academic field have investigated the relationship between corporate governance models and mechanisms and organizations' performance through different perspectives (Coles et al., 2001; Heracleous, 2001; Demsetz and Villalonga, 2001; Bhagat and Jefferies, 2002). Although no quantified impact has been identified in the relationship between the two entities, these studies show that corporate governance matters significantly to a firm's performance, market value and reputation, and thus underline the importance of adopting adequate corporate governance models and principles. Furthermore, it becomes important for companies also to assess their corporate governance policy and practice in an international perspective and against an evolving scenario (Aras and Crowther, 2008).

The mainstream in corporate governance research has been its investigation through the lens of agency theory, which configures the corporation as a nexus of contracts between principals – shareholders, and agents – managers. If we refer to modern firms, the separation of ownership and control is very common (Berle and Means, 1932). In this situation, realigning the interest of principals and agents requires various mechanisms (Fama and Jensen, 1983; Jensen and Meckling, 1976). On the one hand, shareholders aim to maximize their capital returns for a weighted risk and on the other hand, managers may focus more on performance growth and may make costly decisions in terms of products, processes and operations in general. Consequently, agency costs arise because shareholders may not be able to monitor the management properly, and the need for mechanisms to minimize agency problems increases hand-in-hand with them. When this model is applied to different cultures and contexts, the resulting corporate governance prerogatives are dissimilar and are not always captured by the principal-agent framework. Usually studies of corporate governance identify two dichotomous models: the Anglo-American and the Continental European one. "... *The Anglo-American model is also labelled the outsider, common law, market-oriented, shareholder-centred, or liberal model, and the Continental model the insider, civil law, blockholder, bank-oriented, stakeholder-centred, coordinated, or "Rhineland" model ...*" [23]. This differentiation, according to Aguilera and Jackson (2003), is due to the fact that corporate governance should be conceptualized in terms of its embeddedness in different social contexts. They argue that the agency theory, when ap-

---

[23] Aguilera R.V., Jackson G., *The cross-national diversity of corporate governance: Dimensions and determinants*, Academy of management Review, 28(3), 447-465, 2003, p. 447.

plied to corporate governance models studied in different contests, reflects an under-socialized view of corporate governance.

Theoretical assumptions within agency theory focus on the relationship between principal and agent without considering the connotations of their interests defined by the different identities the two parties may have. Furthermore, agency theory omits important interdependencies among other stakeholders in the firm (Freeman, 1984) because of its exclusive focus on the bilateral contracts between principals and agents – "a dyadic reductionism" (Emirbayer and Goodwin, 1994), leaving out, for example, the relationships generated by market institutions. If it excludes these relationships, agency theory may have difficulties in defining the institutional interdependence and complementarities of corporate governance (Parkinson et al., 2001). "... Hence, corporate governance is ultimately the outcome of interactions among multiple stakeholders. For instance, markets for corporate control may serve shareholders by reducing unprofitable investments, but they may also face resistance from employees who fear breaches of trust concerning their firm-specific investments ..." [24]. This can be also reductive if we consider the institutional environment influencing corporate governance (Lubatkin et al., 2001). If priority is given to shareholder rights, the firm's relations with its different environments in the overall system may be ignored, and in actual fact the shareholders' behaviour itself is underestimated, as the model only reflects some of the patterns they are embedded in, and as a consequence only some of their actions. As we saw in the previous paragraphs, firms operating in their overall system enact multiple patterns of parties and their exchanges, originating from different environments. Agency costs are unable to capture their dynamism and their synergic conduct.

Another traditional approach in corporate governance gives exclusive priority to residual claimants in the firm's value maximization process [25]. The crucial element in this analysis is the notion of "residual claimant", commonly known as the part or constituency, who is entitled to obtain benefits from the firm only after all other claims have been satisfied. Under this principle, the only need for the firm is to identify the corporate constituency that holds the residual claim on it. This residual claim must be maximised for the firm's trustees. By definition, in normal situations, there

---

[24] Aguilera R.V., Jackson, G., *The cross-national diversity of corporate governance: Dimensions and determinants*, Academy of management Review, 2003, 28(3), 447-465, p. 449.

[25] Williamson O.E., *Organization form, residual claimants, and corporate control*, The Journal of Law and Economics, 26(2) 351-366, 1983; Fama, E.F., Jensen, M.C., *Agency problems and residual claims*, The Journal of Law and Economics, 26(2), 327-349, 1983.

can be only one residual claimant: the shareholder, and the creditors in the event of insolvency. From this point of view, shareholders are the only constituency whose interests are at risk and dependent on the firm's performance. The other constituencies (such as employees, suppliers, customers, etc.) have defined claims whose values are known in advance or at least in terms of expectations.

The justification for giving primacy to shareholders' interests is that this leads to efficient outcomes, because it requires corporate decision-makers to maximize the residual claims on the company and thus the welfare of the entire corporation and the general community. There are also practical reasons for preferring the shareholder approach, since it can be seen as an efficient, workable rule, as against a rule that considers several, complex classes of constituencies.

This analysis conceals the implicit assumption that, apart from the residual claim, all other claims on the firm are fixed and well defined[26]. Therefore, any other claims, such as the interests and expectations of other individuals or groups, are implicitly considered in the analysis. Thus, the only claim that has to be considered is the residual claim assigned to shareholders. This finding is logical if we consider that the context of reference in which the shareholder-maximizing firm developed was primarily American society in times when financial capital was the scarce resource required to permit the creation of large firms able to benefit from mass markets[27]. But if we contextualise firms' exchanges within the overall system, the business makes use of other vital resources or critical assets supplied by different categories of stakeholders. One concrete example is provided by the many studies that consider knowledge to be a decisive asset for gaining competitive advantage. The owners of these resources can also claim their property rights, in exactly the same way as the financial investors who invested their resources (mainly equity) to create and/or sustain the firm. These parties can also be identified as the individuals or groups with an ongoing interest in the firm's economic and overall sustainability, and which contribute to it through valued assets and resources needed for it to be successful in its operations.

Under the stakeholder approach, firms attempt to maximize and provide for the joint welfare of all the different parties, and to satisfy their often conflicting interests on the basis of the framework established by the firm's corporate governance. In contrast with the shareholder maximization

[26] Licht A., *The Maximands of Corporate Governance: A Theory of Values and Cognitive Style*, Delaware Journal of Corporate Law, 29, 649, 2004.

[27] Chandler Jr. A.D., *The visible hand: The managerial revolution in American business*, Harvard University Press, 1993.

model, not all stakeholders seek to maximize the same values. This is because the resources that each of them brings to the firm and their expectations concerning its operation vary in nature. Employees, for example, according to Kochan and Rubinstein (2000), may expect to balance their short term financial returns against their interest in long-term employment security or their interest in fair treatment against a challenging working experience[28]. From the corporate governance point of view, the problem then is not one of maximizing a single factor but of simultaneously optimizing several factors of different kind, already identified in corporate governance literature some time ago (Freeman and Reed, 1983, Freeman, 1984, 2010, Evan and Freeman, 1988, Donaldson and Preston, 1995). It is difficult to identify a clear overall framework with suitable propositions for practitioners and for empirical testing, which simultaneously balances the needs and resources of different stakeholders. But it is fundamental since, as already described in detail, several studies[29] have shown that the relationships between firms and non-shareholder subjects may be critical for businesses' performance. If these relationships are not considered and if the holders of these interests do not have sufficient incentives and adequate rewards, they may leave and thereby take some of the firm's assets and values with them, making its survival uncertain. In some cases, stakeholders' contribution is critical for both firms' and stakeholders' sustainability, especially in the long run. Their inputs have become integral to firms' strategies and decision-making, even if this implies further expansion and challenging of the corporate governance model.

---

[28] Kochan T.A., Rubinstein S.A., *Toward a stakeholder theory of the firm: The Saturn partnership*, Organization science, 11(4), 367-386, 2000.

[29] Berman S.L., Wicks A.C., Kotha S., Jones T.M., *Does stakeholder orientation matter? The relationship between stakeholder management models and firm financial performance*, Academy of Management journal, 42(5), 488-506, 1999; Clarkson M.E., *A stakeholder framework for analyzing and evaluating corporate social performance*, Academy of management review, 20(1), 92-117, 1995; Perrini F., Tencati A., *Sustainability and stakeholder management: the need for new corporate performance evaluation and reporting systems*, Business Strategy and the Environment, 15(5), 296-308, 2006.

Figure 4. Shareholder vs Stakeholder approach.

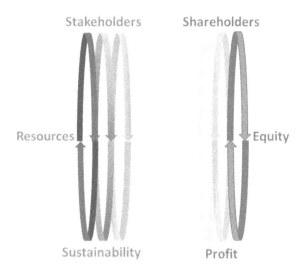

Therefore, in order to manage their increased level of responsibility and accountability to their stakeholders, corporations establish inclusive corporate governance models and develop appropriate governance processes oriented towards stakeholder management and sustainability. Operatively, the corporate governance models that consider broader categories of stakeholders can be identified by applying the parties – contributions – rewards conceptual scheme, (Airoldi et al., 1995). Models of this kind are able to trace structured relationships between stakeholders that provide their resources to the firm in return for rewards and benefits that meet their needs and expectations (Figure 4) and also fit the patterns of the firm's social and economic dimension. The nature of these patterns and their dynamic in space and time can be used to identify appropriate inclusive corporate governance models. A more precise representation (both visual and descriptive) of this conceptual framework will be presented in the following sections.

1.4.2. The role of communities, culture and values in the firm's management

When stakeholder management is implemented in the firm's activities, it enacts organizational design factors and interactions with the constituent parts of the firm's environment and develops a set of shared values and norms of behaviour that constitute the firm's culture (Schein, 2006). A specific issue for stakeholder management is how to combine and integrate both the social and the economic dimensions, conciliating competing norms and values of communities in which firms operates.

An important distinction between the concept of society and community is proposed by one of the "founding fathers" of modern sociology, Ferdinand Tönnies in his work *Gemeinschaft und Gesellschaft* – Community and Civil Society (first published in 1887), a classic of social theory in the later-modern period. It focuses on the common clash between small-scale, kinship and neighbourhood-based "communities" and large-scale competitive market "societies"[30]. This topic is explored in his work in many aspects of life and in particular in political, economic, legal and family structures. According to Tönnies, the most common sense "...ordinary human "Society" we understand simply as individuals living alongside but independently of one another...On the other hand, everyone who praises rural life has pointed to the fact that people there have a stronger and livelier sense of Community. Community means genuine, enduring life together, whereas Society is a transient and superficial thing ..."[31]. Thus, Community must be understood as a living organism in its own right, while society is a mechanical aggregate and artefact.

The firm interacts at both levels, since it engages in exchanges with the society on a wide scale through the markets and institutions in which it competes and with the community at an intermediate level through the local contexts in which it operates. This fact is reported by the growing stream of research that focuses on how both local competitive and market-based processes influence organizations (Audia, Freeman and Reynolds, 2006; Stuart and Sorensen, 2007)[32].

This two-way process can foster the creation of mutual knowledge and experience and may provide firms with knowledge, contacts and resources. The analysis at this point will focus on those exchanges that refer to local communities as one of the main drivers that defines social dimension's patterns. These exchanges create value for both entities as value is obtained through the way the firm attracts tangible and intangible contributions from the community, but value is also produced by the establishment of the firm and grounded in its contribution to the local communities in terms of

---

[30] It is interesting to note the explicit references to Aristotle in Community and Civil Society in Tönnies's representation of small-scale communities as a natural outgrowth of the autochthonous household "Οἰκονομικά" – Economics.

[31] Tönnies F., Harris J., *Community and civil society*, Vol. 266, Cambridge: Cambridge University Press, 2001, p. 19.

[32] For a complete review on this topic refer to: Marquis C., Battilana J., 2009, *Acting globally but thinking locally? The enduring influence of local communities on organizations*, Research in organizational behavior, 29, 283-302; Audia P.G., Freeman, J.H., Reynolds, P.D., *Organizational foundings in community context: Instruments manufacturers and their interrelationship with other organizations*, Administrative Science Quarterly, 51(3), 381-419, 2006.

the general welfare it produces through its products and service, employment, etc. Therefore, a circular process is identified in the patterns that link firms to their community – drawing from the local community and giving to the local community.

Many factors concerning local communities are fundamental for understanding organizations and their actions (Marquis and Battilana, 2009; Marquis, Glynn, and Davis, 2007; Sorge, 2005). Marquis and Battilana (2009) identify and analyse three principal mechanisms through which communities can influence organizational behaviour: "... local communities are institutional arenas that have an enduring influence on organizational behaviour through regulative, normative, and cultural-cognitive processes ..." [33]. The regulatory and legal structures of the communities may involve formal rules and incentives that may induce organizations to implement specific managerial practices. One example is the local public policies based on incentives such as subsidies to industry, tax breaks, infrastructure facilities, and labour training programs. Similarly, organizational practices may be influenced by social-normative processes, in which organizations answer to the expectations of community's actors in order to obtain their approval. In this conceptualization of social-normative mechanisms, the authors focus on how local relational systems identity different standards of appropriateness across communities (Marquis and Battilana, 2009). The social-normative concept is based on the idea that local social factors lead organizations to guide their behaviour in accordance to what is seen as socially appropriate in a given the context. Communities also have a set of shared frameworks or mental models upon which its members use for when evaluating a situation. "... Cultural-cognitive institutional forces are pervasive frames of reference and identity that provide templates or models that facilitate the adoption of similar practices for members of a community group ..." [34].

The main elements that identify and enable the distinctiveness of a given community in the way it influences management processes, are its cultural and values. Cultural values within the organization are likely to affect the level of integration of the two dimensions – economic and social – within the organizational design and management.

In one of the most widely cited studies in management literature, the Global Leadership and Organizational Behaviour Effectiveness (GLOBE) project defines culture as "shared motives, values, beliefs, identities, and

---

[33] Marquis C., Battilana J., *Acting globally but thinking locally? The enduring influence of local communities on organizations*, Research in organizational behavior, 29, 283-302, 2009, p. 294.

[34] *Ibidem*, p. 292.

interpretations or meanings of significant events that result from common experiences of members of collectives that are transmitted across generations"[35]. This definition proposes common values and shared meanings as important factors for identifying cultural groups. Scholars generally agree that variations between groups can exist on multiple levels as firms are simultaneously embedded in multiple environments but most studies have focused only on the organizational field levels of analysis (Battilana, 2006). Furthermore, studies that consider culture-related issues in organizational behaviour use a variety of cultural dimensions along with many different measures. The most frequent topics in the review proposed by Tsui et al., (2007) are ethical orientation, negotiation, conflict management, and team behaviour and processes[36].

According to these studies, cultural values have a clear relationship with managerial values in decision-making at the firm level. They maintain that societal-level values (such as community/state values) can be predictive of the values held at the firm level (Waldman et al 2006). Members of a given culture can influence the specific values and beliefs relevant to the firm's functioning and its decision-making process. According to these relationships, the values identified in a given cultural context influence the managerial values adopted at a firm level in decision-making processes. The influence of culture in management processes is extensively investigated, especially in the case of corporate social responsibility and in particular in the processes that directly impact CSR decisions.

Moreover, according to stakeholder theory, managerial values can be classified and subdivided into three main categories (Waldman et al 2006). The first refers to the shareholder approach, meaning the values assigned to tasks in relation to shareholders or owners to maximise profits – economic responsibility. The second relates to ethical and positive values concerning stakeholders' interests – social and environmental responsibility. The last consists of values related to a broader entity such as the community/state. This third dimension reflects values such as philanthropy, referring to responsibility for public welfare, and involves wider societal entities such as the community (Wood, 1991). During its operations, the firm can benefit from long-term relationships built on implicit accords or shared values in all these three dimensions, which may resolve situations not covered by contracts.

---

[35] House R.J., et al. (ed.). *Culture, leadership, and organizations: The GLOBE study of 62 societies*, Sage publications, 2004, p. 15.

[36] Tsui A.S., Nifadkar S.S., Ou A.Y., *Cross-national, cross-cultural organizational behavior research: Advances, gaps, and recommendations*, Journal of management, 33(3), 426-478, 2007.

Figure 5. Community and values in the firm's management.

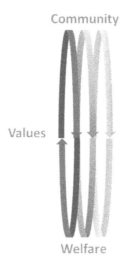

Community

Values

Welfare

To sum up, culture is an important source of values that facilitate the adoption of similar practices for members of a community group and can provide templates or models that define firm's decision-making and management activities. Due to the variety of areas in which culture can be translated into the management field, it should be analysed at a multidimensional level. In the general scheme represented in Figure 5, the focus is on the broadest level – the community/state culture – as shareholder and stakeholder cultural values are intrinsic to each of these two groups and are encompassed in the specific contributions represented by their different categories of patterns.

Furthermore, culture is also important at an operating level, in particular when corporate decision-makers consider which strategies to adopt, grounding their decisions in the cultural environment where they are developed and bearing in mind how public opinion would respond to the possible courses of action. This may happen in particular in situations where pressure is high, when several options need to be weighed and managers are expected to be held accountable for their decisions. In these conditions, especially, under increased pressure to reach decisions, people resort to their shared implicit cultural knowledge[37]. That is the reason why people from different cultures perceive, understand and judge firms' socially orient-

---

[37] Licht, A.N., Goldschmidt C., Schwartz S.H., Culture rules: *The foundations of the rule of law and other norms of governance*, Journal of comparative economics, 35(4), 659-688, 2007.

ed activities and performance in different ways. Decision-making will thus be affected by the general culture of the community in which firm operates.

These facts are particularly relevant to the social dimension of the firm and the patterns of exchanges identified within its community which are established and driven by cultural values.

1.4.3. The role of market and competition in firms' management

In the case of the economic dimension, market-based processes can define important criteria that influence competitiveness factors for firms operating in a large-scale institutional construct – the competitive market. At the same time, the market's equilibrium is itself defined by firms' inputs, provided through their performance and behaviour related to market conditions. The rules and conditions defined in a given market are one of the most important components of firms' overall systems, as they guide the setting up of the firms' decision-making processes. In this exchange between firms and the markets, companies can also interact proactively with markets' competitive behaviours. From a managerial perspective, it is important to analyze how the resources in the patterns relating to market institutions can be managed given the market's institutional framework. Important examples of the influence that firms' behaviour may have on market efficiency and how they can benefit from the management of their behaviour toward the market are provided by signalling theory.

Figure 6. Patterns of the firm's economic dimension.

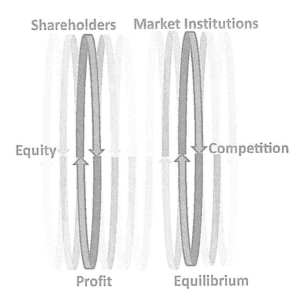

Management research has made functional contributions to the application and understanding of the complex signalling processes that occur between two entities in the presence of asymmetrical information [38]. For long time, economic models of decision-making processes were based on the assumption of perfect information, where such information asymmetries were ignored (Stiglitz, 2002). In spite of the notorious information imperfections, economists had generally assumed that markets with minor imperfections would behave substantively the same as markets with perfect information, but Stiglitz (2000) pinpoints two broad categories of information where asymmetry is especially important: information about quality and information about intent. The concept of quality is particularly important as it refers to "… the underlying, unobservable ability of the signaller to fulfil the needs or demands of an outsider observing the signal …" [39]. The mainstream of management studies that explicitly invoke signalling theory focus on the role of signalling in understanding how parties resolve information asymmetries about latent and unobservable quality of information (Connelly et al., 2011).

Preannouncing potential behaviour is a form of market signalling. More specifically "… competitive market signals are announcements or previews of potential actions intended to convey information or to gain information from competitors …" [40]. Therefore, competitive behaviour may be influenced by signals sent by competitors and the efficiency of the market can be increased considerably if competitors can read signals effectively before they act. Example of signals include the preannouncements of new products and services, projection of price increases or decreases, market entry or exit, capacity increases, and future changes in advertising levels.

In order to put adequate signalling strategies in place, the company, when is the signal sender, must make several decisions – whether or not send the signal, when to send it, and to whom the signal should be addressed. Operatively, the basic rationale for competitive market signalling is that the benefits to the organization – signal sender of increased leverage or increased information must exceed the potential costs (Heil and Robertson, 1991).

---

[38] A complete review of signalling theory use in the management literature is provided in Connelly B.L., Certo S.T., Ireland R.D., Reutzel C.R., *Signaling theory: A review and assessment*, Journal of Management, 37(1), 39-67, 2011.

[39] Connelly B.L., Certo S.T., Ireland R.D., Reutzel C.R., *Signaling theory: A review and assessment*, Journal of Management, 37(1), 39-67, 2011, p. 43.

[40] Heil O., Robertson T.S., *Toward a theory of competitive market signaling: A research agenda*, Strategic Management Journal, 12(6), 403-418, 1991, p. 403.

1.5. Representation of the firm's social dimension

Putting together the concepts investigated and developed so far, which, in different ways and from different perspectives, are all related to and can foster the firm's social dimension and its influence on management infrastructure and processes, enables us to visualise the set of patterns that are its determinants. If we consider the patterns of parties – contributions – rewards, two main categories emerge. The main one considers the inclusive approach for the firm's management of its stakeholders, with all the types of resources they bring to the firm and their expectations concerning the outcome of its business and its impact in terms of economic, social and environmental performance. This concept is often reported by considering the patterns of single groups of stakeholders who contribute different kinds of resources and the receive the relative rewards, in order to determine the value of a company from the perspective of single categories of stakeholder (such as customers, employees, environment, etc.), by assessing the value of each group and its resources – rewards to the company or vice versa. This approach is effective for evaluating the firm's social dimension as it encompasses and tackles the combination of resources and expectations of several stakeholder groups at the same time. Similarly, when developing a method for evaluating corporate social responsibility, Schaltegger and Figge (2000) propose the concept of Stakeholder Value Added, which allows all a company's stakeholder relations to be evaluated on the basis of the value of stakeholder relationships from the firm's perspective. But since it focuses on the firm's performance, it fragments the patterns that relate the stakeholders to the rewards they obtain from the firm's activities.

If we shift attention from the parties to the resources that the firm manages in its activities, one specific category – cultural values – emerges as clearly separate from the stakeholders' resources, as it can influence the firm's management at different levels and from different perspectives. Cultural values can be controlled by parties that represent different groups of stakeholders at the same time (such as the community), and the outputs sought by these parties are broader, embracing multilevel results in terms of the welfare of the overall system, including the performance of all levels of business activities and the impacts produced for the firm, stakeholders and community. As a result, a further category of patterns related to the dynamics of community – values – welfare exchanges can emerge within the firm's social dimension. The more the firm is internationalized and interacts with different cultures, the more these patterns are evident and the more important it becomes to consider and analyse them in the specific overall system in which the social dimension is configured.

Figure 7. Patterns of the firm's social dimension.

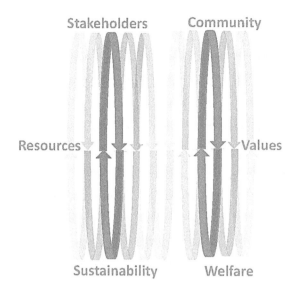

The representation of the patterns of the firm's social dimension, considered jointly with those of its economic dimension, can be useful in figuring out appropriate inclusive corporate governance models and in multidimensional performance evaluation. When identifying the governance model, it is usually crucial to consider the principal parties that have a "stake" in the running of the firm, focusing on their dyadic relationships, with their rights considered at different levels. In this picture, the resources provided to the firm are defined basically with reference to the parties that contribute them to the business activities or by considering the hierarchy of categories of interests in the firm that guide its management choices. In this process, all the components of the social dimension patterns are considered, but by means of the dyadic relations that run through these three entities, without taking into account their overall dynamics and the synergies between economic and social dimension patterns. By applying the proposed perspective, based on the dynamic and synergies of the patterns within the two dimensions, it is possible not only to identify the "actors" in corporate governance, but also to consider their links to various contributions and their multiple interests embodied in the firm's management (economic and social, short and long term). Accurate identification of these patterns and the analysis of their evolution within the firm's overall system can help managers to pinpoint appropriate inclusive governance models and at the same time to establish the right prerogatives for management processes implemented using them.

Chapter 2

THE SOCIAL DIMENSION IN THE FIRM'S MANAGEMENT

SUMMARY: 2.1. Corporate Social Responsibility in the firm's social dimension. – 2.2. Operationalizing Corporate Social Strategy. – 2.3. Communication within the firm's social dimension. – 2.3.1. Non-financial disclosure. – 2.3.2. CSR communication. – 2.4. A theoretical framework for managing social and economic dimension patterns. – 2.5. Managing the social dimension for innovation. – 2.5.1. Managing social innovation through the firm's social dimension. – 2.6. Crisis management through the lens of the social dimension framework. – 2.6.1. Communicating crises to stakeholders.

A framework or approach giving due consideration to social dimension patterns would allow companies to assess their business in terms of Corporate Social Responsibility (CSR) on a company – and project-specific level. It could facilitate the further implementation of socially oriented activities and performance and support effective decision-making processes.

2.1. Corporate Social Responsibility in the firm's social dimension

Defining the firm's social dimension focuses attention on stakeholder and resource patterns that are already part of managerial decision-making processes even though they are not always formally recognised in governance and management models. While the management of economic recourses is highly formalized in terms of models, tools and processes, social and environmental resources have traditionally been treated as peripheral to corporate strategy and disclosed by companies on voluntary bases. But as previous studies, especially those on Corporate Social Responsibility, underline, social and environmental performance can be translated into long-term shareholder value when firms ensure that the associated activities are fully integrated into strategic processes (Adams and McNicholas, 2007; Porter and Kramer, 2011).

The application of the CSR approach to the management field began in the 1950s and is claimed to have been fully explored in the 1990s (Drucker, 1993). In particular, the question of why some companies perform their business better than others stimulated a broad range of strategic management research, including CSR-based studies. The strategic management field that analyses stakeholder management has also investigated CSR issues in both theoretical and empirical terms. The corporate social responsibility approach that applies stakeholder theory has been developed primarily by business management scholars, encouraged by the lack of practical applications in social and environmental activities and the gaps in performance measurement of the other traditional profit-oriented perspectives. This approach may solve the problem of measuring the social contribution to the firm's performance by pinpointing the main players involved in firms and defining their resources and functions in relation to each other within management activities. From the managers' perspective, their responsibilities towards employees, customers and government can be identified easily, as they are part of the management construct. In addition, most companies, intentionally or unintentionally, have already managed these relationships as a fundamental part of their operations, through their interactions with their environment systems. Therefore, in this field data can easily be retraced from management activities. Following this approach, in one of the first and most widely cited studies on CSR Clarkson (1995) applies the stakeholder model to CSR research. Based on his experience of empirical research into this topic, he attempts to revise the stakeholder model to better adapt it to the needs of the CSR approach. Firstly, he argues that it is necessary to distinguish between stakeholder needs and social issues where these are defined as substantial public issues to the extent that legal norms or other forms of regulation are necessary. If no such legislation or regulation applies, it is possible to talk about issues related to stakeholders, but not necessarily to social problems. Once the nature of problems has been identified, Clarkson argues that it is necessary to define the appropriate levels of analysis concerning their characteristics (institutional, organizational and individual). Only then can managers analyse and evaluate the company's social performance. Following this method, he also added new measurement tools to the CSR approach [1].

The above are only a few of the first studies in the field of CSR but there are several other important works that have contributed to the debate, and have been discussed in an equally large number of works reviewing CSR research, in different business disciplines [2]. The aim here is to pin-

---

[1] Clarkson M.E.A., Stakeholder *framework for analyzing and evaluating corporate social performance*, Academy of management review, 20(1), 92-117, 1995.

[2] For more details, please refer to: Garriga E., Melé D., *Corporate social responsibility theories: Mapping the territory*, Journal of business ethics, 53(1), 51-71, 2004; Margolis J.D., Walsh J.P., *Misery loves companies: Rethinking social initiatives by business*, Administrative science quarterly, 48(2), 268-305, 2003; McWilliams A., Siegel D., *Corporate social responsibility: A theory of the firm perspective*, Academy of management

point the studies that analyse CSR from the managerial perspective, offering operative implications for firms implementing social oriented strategies. Despite the broad sharing of CSR issues, the literature referred to offers very few tools for the management, control and evaluation of the interaction between the social and economic dimensions of CSR activities, in particular.

As the historical and conceptual evolution of corporate social responsibility issues and the "natural selection" of operational CSR activities clearly reveal, the most widely accepted approach seems to tend towards the strategic conceptualization of CSR. In this regard, the Green Paper "Promoting a European Corporate Social Responsibility Framework" (2001) of the Commission of the European Communities defines the concept of social responsibility as "… a concept whereby companies integrate social and environmental concerns in their business operations and in their interaction with their stakeholders on a voluntary basis …"[3], pointing out the new expectations and new stakeholders to be taken into account in firms' management and the growing influence that social dimensions have on business activities and vice versa. In view of these and other reasons, although the company's main area of responsibility continues to be economic, the Green Paper reiterates that "… companies can at the same time contribute to social and environmental objectives, through integrating corporate social responsibility as a strategic investment into their core business strategy, their management instruments and their operations …"[4], confirming the integration of CSR into strategy and business activities once again.

In the same way, studies of CSR that focus on environmental issues add to the concept of sustainability and argue that, considering the immense environmental challenges the world faces today, if the concept of sustainability is included in their strategies or technological development, businesses can obtain a significant competitive advantage (Schaltegger et al, 2017). CSR management is actually very similar to corporate sustainability management, which aims to integrate the economic, environmental, and social aspects of business management and is described as "business's contribution to sustainable development" by the OECD[5]. The aim of corporate

review, 26(1), 117-127, 200; Scherer A.G., Palazzo G., *The new political role of business in a globalized world: A review of a new perspective on CSR and its implications for the firm, governance, and democracy*, Journal of management studies, 48(4), 899-931, 2011.

[3] European Commission. Directorate General for Employment, *Promoting a European Framework for Corporate Social Responsibility: Green Paper*, Office for Official Publications of the European Communities, DOC 01/9, 18 July, 2001, p. 6.

[4] *Ibidem*, p. 4.

[5] OECD, *Corporate social responsibility: Partners for progress*, Paris, OECD, 2001, p. 13.

sustainability is the integration of all three sustainability components (economics, social and environmental) into business management processes, which can even lead to changes in the business model in order to pursue sustainable operations in a long-term perspective (Weber, 2008). CSR and corporate sustainability can therefore be considered as sub areas encompassed in the broader framework of firm's social dimension.

In line with previous studies, Lockett et al., (2006) identify CSR as a field of study within management, with highly permeable boundaries, that "... exhibit a number of different research traditions focusing on different issues relating to CSR ..."[6]. Benefits for firms deriving from CSR and sustainability activities have been analysed in both theoretical and empirical research[7]. But even though many of these studies analyses the economic success as a possible outcome of CSR management, it was not always considered as a key issue.

As a result of these developments, traceable in the academic literature and tested by operative findings, a practical evolution can be identified, parallel to the theoretical development process, in which CSR is growing in importance and becoming highly integrated into strategic management.

In the strategic management literature[8] in particular, it is widely accepted that competitive advantage requires, among other inputs and capabilities, a fit between the external environment and firms' strategic actions. The firm's social dimension is therefore an important source for defining appropriate strategic management, with the aim of pursuing competitive advantage. Furthermore, strategic decision-making, it is argued, is driven by top management's values, which include commitment to both economic and social responsibility (Husted and Allen, 2007). The goal of strategic management is the creation of competitive advantage, which brings value creation, through the ability to properly manage the whole process performed, considering the firm's interaction within its overall system. In particular, value can be created when potential beneficiaries are willing to pay an additional amount for the firm's products and services after evaluating its involvement in and contribution to the specific social issues it deals with. Following this application of CSR, the relationship between CSR ac-

---

[6] Lockett A., Moon J., Visser W., *Corporate social responsibility in management research: Focus, nature, salience and sources of influence*, Journal of management studies, 43(1), 115-136, 2006, p. 117.

[7] A review can be found in Weber M., *The business case for corporate social responsibility: A company-level measurement approach for CSR*, European Management Journal, 26(4), 247-261, 2008.

[8] Grant R.M., *Contemporary Strategy Analysis: Concepts, Techniques, Applications*, Blackwell Publishers, Oxford, 2005.

tivities and corporate economic performance has been developed in terms of both its theoretical and its practical implications in many strategic management studies such as McWilliams and Siegel (2001), Kotler and Lee (2005), Porter and Kramer (2006; 2011) and Martin (2002). In efforts to trace the strategic implications of corporate social responsibility, the focus is on the work of researchers attempting to eliminate the gap between social and economic performance. In these studies, the two concepts are tightly related and closely integrated.

McWilliams and Siegel (2001) outline a supply and demand model of CSR, arguing that a firm's level of CSR will depend on many factors related to its activities, such as size, level of diversification, research and development, marketing, government, sales, consumer income, labour market conditions, and stage in the industry life cycle[9]. According to this conceptualization, in order to maximize profit, the firm needs to offer exactly the "ideal" level of CSR at which the increased revenue deriving from higher demand that compensates the higher costs incurred for CSR activities. In this way, the firm can efficiently meet the demands of both shareholders and the relevant stakeholders. Suggesting that there is a neutral relationship between CSR and financial performance, the study maintains that managers can determine this "ideal" level of CSR via cost-benefit analysis. On the one hand managers will have to evaluate the possibility of product/service differentiation, while on the other they will need to evaluate the resource costs of promoting CSR and pinpoint the possible scale and/or scope economies linked to the CSR actions undertaken.

Another important contribution is Martin's Virtue Matrix (2002), a framework made up of four quadrants for assessing opportunities for socially responsible behaviour, which sets out to determine whether a particular corporate action benefited shareholders, society, both, or neither. The two quadrants placed at the bottom of the matrix make up the foundation of civil society (the "common law" of responsible corporate behaviour) and the top two its frontier. The bottom left quadrant contains the actions that corporations engage in by choice, in accordance with norms and customs. The bottom right quadrant represents actions undertaken in compliance with laws or regulations. The top two quadrants of the matrix, named the strategic and structural frontiers, include activities the motivations of which are more intrinsic. The left one, named the strategic frontier, includes activities that may produce value for shareholders thanks to the positive reactions from customers, employees, or other stakeholders. Finally,

---

[9] McWilliams A., Siegel D., *Corporate social responsibility: A theory of the firm perspective*, Academy of management review, 26(1), 117-127, 2001.

the upper right quadrant of the matrix (the structural frontier), hosts activities that are still intrinsically encouraged but that are clearly contrary to the interests of shareholders. The corporate actions reported in this quadrant increase benefits for stakeholders and society rather than for the firm.

The virtue matrix was designed to help managers in their efforts to meet stakeholders' social expectations and offers a framework for evaluating their claims, but it still does not solve or eliminate the competing claims of shareholders and society.

Another field of application for CSR was proposed by Kotler and Lee (2005), who developed a complex picture explaining why CSR activities are useful to businesses in the marketing realm. Considering a specific branch of CSR – "corporate social marketing" (CSM) – they analyse the CSR strategy that uses marketing principles and practices to foster changes in customers' behaviour, improving social performance while building new markets for products or services.

Finally, Porter and Kramer (2011) encourage companies to become farsighted in their "philanthropic costs", because expenditure in this area has the potential to become valuable investments that can support the underlying business background. They argue that adopting strategic CSR offers new opportunities for innovation, explores new, previously unknown markets, and develops into precious social relationships that can help the business with its reputation. Explaining their shared value conceptualization, they explain that forward-looking businesses want to be part of the solution to tackling the complex problems facing society. Companies are aware of socially oriented activities such as those included in corporate social responsibility. However, firms should expand their engagement in society so that their core business models can improve the well-being of people and the planet, and reduce or eliminate negative externalities while earning profits. Externalities arise when firms create social costs that they do not have to bear, such as pollution. Thus, governments must impose taxes, norms, and punishments so that firms "internalize" these externalities. In these conditions, Corporate Responsibility programmes are seen as an answer to this pressure and are proposed with the aim of improving firms' reputations, and are classified as a necessary expense (Porter and Kramer, 2011). Advancing the concept of shared value, Porter finds that social harms or weaknesses can often generate internal costs for firms, such as wasted energy and raw resources, costly accidents, etc. CSR's inclusion in firms' management does not necessarily raise costs for firms but can actually increase their productivity and expand their markets if it is used to innovate through the adoption of new technologies, operating methods, and management approaches.

Summing up, managing CSR in a profit-return process is just like managing traditional market activities. It can be done by redefining non-market social activities as profitable goods and services (Porter and Kramer 2011). Strategic management of non-market social activities can turn what is considered an expense into an investment with a measurable potential return (Husted and Allen, 2007).

2.2. Operationalizing Corporate Social Strategy

If social responsibility activities are recognized at a strategic level, it is necessary to locate firms' social dimension within a long-term process that can be identified in their vision statements, to guide the whole organization's activities within its overall system. A strategy therefore has to be adopted that includes both the social and the economic dimensions, in order to plan the allocation of resources to meet long-term objectives. This process is similar to and can be implemented within the traditional business strategy, or in some cases, by developing analogous ad hoc social strategies. Social strategy can therefore be defined as "… *the kind of decision-making that seeks to achieve social goals, to provide value added to its environment and to achieve the maximum coincidence between the values of the company and those of its social groups of interests, with the aim of obtaining a competitive advantage through the consensus and legitimation, even in the context of the indispensable economic equilibrium maintenance …*" [10]. This definition takes into account the concept represented in Porter's and Kramer's (2011) studies of strategic CSR, and positions strategic decisions as part of the social dimension within inclusive governance.

Following this approach, strategies regarding firms' social dimension go through a process of elaboration that can be divided into five main phases. In an initial analysis, social objectives are related to economic ones at a general level, identifying the extent of the social dimension the company intends to incorporate into its management structure through its exchanges and relationships with its environment. To move on to the implementation of these goals, firms have to adapt them to their own specific stakeholders and processes in order to make them measurable. Secondly, the process goes hand in hand with the elaboration of the strategy, in which the main trends must be linked to the social dimension, to ensure that the economic activity offers stakeholders alternative solutions for achieving the social goals set. Next comes the operational phase of the strategy, during which

---

[10] Chirieleison C., *Le strategie sociali nel governo dell'azienda*, Giuffrè, Milano, 2002, pp. 94-95.

investment, financing and economic and social indicators are defined. Alongside the general formulation of the prospected performance and its measurement, the process must identify the single activities with the corresponding budget and other indicators useful for controlling and evaluating their ongoing and ex post performance. These indicators are also crucial for the auditing process, where the results are compared with those set in the firm's goals, and can help in taking any corrective action and in the revision of future objectives. In a final stage, the activities that led to the achievement of social goals should also be analysed. All surveys and evaluations are contained in documents with quantitative and qualitative content aimed at informing the stakeholders to whom the activities are addressed about the social and economic performance achieved by the firm as a result of the inclusion of social dimension issues in its corporate strategy.

Hence, we can affirm that the implementation of social strategies implies a process in which the firm makes precise choices about the levels of its social dimension, within which it sets it goals and commits its resources, creating a hierarchy of these patterns of relationships for its management framework, in order to be able to optimize its economic and social performance in the long run.

Research is therefore required to understand the role of management infrastructures in facilitating the management of social and environmental activities that can support the achievement of the firm's overall objectives (Gond et al., 2012; Perez et al., 2007). This also highlights the importance of greater understanding of the internal management processes through which the social dimension is managed and linked to other business processes.

2.3. Communication within the firm's social dimension

Given the firm's important role in the social and economic context in which it conducts its operations, the need to revise the type and content of traditional business disclosure emerges. First and foremost, disclosure is becoming increasingly important due to the growth in the number and types of stakeholders, arising from the increasing need for the firm to acquire a larger number of external resources and consensuses owned by different parties and fundamental for pursuing organizations' missions. Apart from this growth in terms of the quantity and quality of information, there are also many other variables related to the type of business information.

2.3.1. Non-financial disclosure

Various studies demonstrate that traditional reporting documents – related mainly to corporate accounting and constructed to meet the needs of government and management accounting and to comply with legal reporting requirements – are now inadequate [11]. At a broader level, however, business disclosure, especially in the economic and financial areas, is no longer sufficient to meet all the information needs of the various stakeholders. The accounting documents that are the keystones of firms' economic and financial reporting (the balance sheet, the business plan, the budget and all the other related reports) are no longer sufficient to fulfil the function of informing all stakeholders and capturing and measuring the social consequences of business operations. As a result, new social disclosure tools have emerged to overcome the limitations of financial reporting and provide a broader solution to the already numerous needs corporate reporting is required to satisfy.

Social disclosure must have the same basic aims as traditional economic reporting, namely "… seeking consensus from the widest categories of parties and in particular from those that deal directly or indirectly with the company, having the awareness that the major consensus can be translated into competitiveness factors …" [12]. As in any other disclosure field, for social reporting it is not enough to simply focus on image and reputation-building objectives; it is necessary to demonstrate companies' genuine commitment to their stakeholders and offer something more than a mere public relations activity. In order to make this process efficient, directions need to be identified to enable the information flow to comply with the relevant stakeholders' expectations and thus the business mission. This can be possible by including social communication choices in the decision-making process within the social strategy phases seen in the previous paragraphs. This means, from an operational point of view, that companies should develop "listening skills" in order to recognize the needs and perceptions that stakeholders make available in their exchanges within the overall system, while simultaneously improving their ability to pick up and understand expectations and potential conflicts, in order to identify possible effective solutions. In addition, the communication process must be honest and open, even in critical situations, to enhance to extend the company's transparency and the credibility in the eyes of the various stakeholders (Corvi, 2007).

Given its multidimensionality, social communication plays a key role in the configuration of the company's social dimension, as it is the direct expression of the dynamic of information exchange in the company's patterns

---

[11] Corvi E., *La comunicazione aziendale. Obiettivi, tecniche, strumenti*, Egea, Milano, 2007; Bruni G., Le *informazioni complementari al Bilancio. Quale reporting revolution?*, Rivista italiana di ragioneria e di economia aziendale, n. 1 e 2, 2007, p. 2.

[12] Zavani M., *Il valore della comunicazione aziendale. Rilevanza e caratteri dell'informativa sociale e ambientale*, Giappichelli, Torino, 2000, p. 51.

within its overall system. Broad social communication means involvement of different stakeholder categories and thus gives the company an extensive set of relational patterns within its environment, which can help to outline the configuration of a complex social dimension for the firm.

Referring to the type of information exchange within the social dimension, there are no coded standards for its content. As a result, various models and methods for non-financial disclosure, such as social and environmental reports, codes of ethics, and numerous social responsibility reports, have been adopted by firms all over the world. The information contained in these documents is generally divided according to the different stakeholder needs to which it refers. In most cases, it provides qualitative and quantitative information on the effects of the business activity. Obviously, this information, covers both social and economic outcomes, and therefore refers to different actors and their contributions, but it seldom takes into account the corresponding expectations that they may have concerning the firm's activities. Generally, this information helps companies to share and disseminate their decisions and results, but it can also foster a two-way dialogue with all stakeholders. In order to be effective, the content must be tailored to the purposes of the disclosure and the characteristics and expectations of the stakeholders to whom it is addressed. These features need to be taken into account, especially when using these reporting categories for assessing a company's social performance and managing its social dimension. As social disclosure flows through the different patterns and can influence firms' decision-making processes with regard to their exchanges within the overall system, its features are also important for assessing the firm's social dimension and how it relates to its economic one.

2.3.2. CSR communication

A specific category of firms' non-financial disclosure is CSR communication that can be considered a heterogeneous topic and is investigated in many business disciplines such as management, public relations, marketing and more. The most important literature regarding CSR communications focuses on four main areas (Crane and Glozer, 2016): CSR Integration, Interpretation, Identity an Image. The aim is to direct CSR communications to internal and external stakeholders, mostly, a company's employees, customers, suppliers, etc., with the purpose of communicating specific CSR-related facts. Communicating these issues is essential to involve and integrate all parties in a firm's CSR activities and can help build a general consensus and sense of identity. Another feature of this communication process concerns the influence of language and interpretation of business facts as a way to legitimize CSR initiatives as strictly related also to a specific context values and culture. Being language the vehicle through which culture is communicated, the CSR process heavily depends on the use of different language to better express its numerous fields of action. Another section of studies on CSR focuses on the narrative role of language in the process of sensemaking and building identity. Storytelling, for example, is a key aspect in involving stakeholders, especially internal ones. Narration of both quantitative and qualitative information can create an important connection between people working in a company and the company's or organization's ethics, trigger emotions, involve, provoke or enhance sensibility to particular topics.

Another CSR communication aim is to communicate the company's or organization's identity to all relevant parties for firms' operation. Although the identity of a business can be shaped through its products, mission and vision, or annual reports, other intangible aspects seem to be even more important when trying to create consumer loyalty and above all, stem consumers' scepticism and create a bond between stakeholders, communities and the business. In the field or CSR, good corporate identity can only be achieved when there are no discrepancies between stakeholders' expectations and real company performances (Kiriakidou and Millward, 2000), as these discrepancies can lead to consumers' suspicions. In this last aspect, communications are important to foster transparency when considering a company's behaviour, but it becomes crucial in crisis situations: "... The critical component in crisis management is communication ..." [13].

As bad crisis management can jeopardize a business, a good communication strategy is essential for its survival. Literature on crisis communication provides a wide range of theories and models which can be followed to tackle crisis situations, however, the approach proposed by, seems to better sum up the crisis management techniques applied by companies. The first technique is called "corporate apologia", hence, a set of communication techniques which can restore corporate legitimacy (the consistency between organizational values and stakeholder values) via dissociation (arguing that a person or group within the organization is responsible for the crisis, not the entire organization) or apologia (Coombs, 2010).

Another technique investigated in this realm, is called "image restoration theory /image repair theory" and as the name suggests, it is used in case of attack to a company's reputation. There is a main differentiation to make in both these techniques, that is, the difference between "rhetoric of renewal"

---

[13] Coombs W.T., Holladay S.J., *The handbook of crisis communication* (Vol. 22), John Wiley & Sons, 2011, pp. 17-53.

and "apologia", as this implies the use of different language and content. With "rhetoric of renewal", the emphasis in on a positive view of the organization's future rather than dwelling on the present, while "apologia" aims to restore the violation of stakeholders' expectations with the company's actions.

In its growing importance, CSR communications have over the years been particularly paying attention to communicating the long-term and durable impacts of business on future generations (Funk, 2003). The general aim is to improve the human and natural resources needed for future generations while "thinking strategically and acting proactively to mitigate their negative impacts on the environment and society. Organizations are required to create new patterns, processes and strategies to tackle the complex socio-ecological issues" [14]. This being said, the content of CSR communications can be subdivided into different categories (Henderson, 2001): sustainable development, corporate social performance, corporate citizenship and strategy implementation.

Most CSR communications are carried out via CSR reports or specific sections in firm's web site and are therefore provided by the company itself. Studies have shown that CSR communication via corporate sources will trigger more scepticism and have less credibility than non corporate sources (Du, et al., 2010). However, a counterpart these days is the increasing involvement of third parties: customers, monitoring groups, media, consumer forums and blogs, as main influence in CSR reporting, as they are not directly controlled by the company.

2.4. A theoretical framework for managing social and economic dimension patterns

The constant contra-positioning of the economic and social dimensions of firms' management has emphasised the trade-offs between a firm's social and economic performance. Social improvement has been considered for long time as a constraint to a company that is maximising profits, since it raises its costs (Porter and Kramer, 2011). This perspective has also shaped the strategies of firms themselves, which have largely excluded social and environmental considerations from their economic thinking. "... Firms have taken the broader context in which they do business as a given and resisted regulatory standards as invariably contrary to their interests ..." [15].

---

[14] Funk K., *Sustainability and performance*, MIT Sloan Management Review, 44(2), 65, 2003, p. 42.

[15] Porter M.E., Kramer M.R., *Creating shared value*, Harvard Business Review, 89 (1/2), 62-77, 2011, p. 65.

Solving social problems has been seen as the duty of governments and NGOs and as an externality for companies. As a result, corporate responsibility programs have been treated as an answer to external pressure and have been implemented to improve firms' reputations. Since it is synonymous with unavoidable expenditure, firms have also seen CSR as an irresponsible use of shareholders' recourses. From the contrary perspective, governments have regulated social issues based mainly through the punishment of non-compliant behaviours.

As a result, and as reported previously, an analysis of the progress of research into stakeholder management and CSR today indicates that there is no clear relationship between a firm's social and economic performances. Many firms are aware that social and environmental issues are important to business, but they are still treated at the periphery of companies' management. There are many guidelines and best practices reported in this field that represent potential solutions for firms' social and environmental issues, but they are often viewed as additional costs for the economic dimension of companies. Even though there has been a change in firms' behaviour toward the social and environmental problems their activities may cause, it remains difficult to figure out the entity of firms' effective contribution to the resolution of social and environmental problems and demonstrate the link between firms' social and economic performance.

It seems that at this stage, using the notion of Watzlawick's theory of change (Watzlawick et al., 2011), firms have adopted first-order change in order to respond to corporate social and environmental issues. According to his theory, there are two different types of change: "... one that occurs within a given system which itself remains unchanged, and one whose occurrence changes the system itself ..." [16]. Trying to apply this conceptualization to firms' social dimension issues, first-order change may occur when firms' social and environmental behaviour shifts in a direction which is more responsible and "caring" (as in the case of Corporate philanthropic and CSR activities) in the attempt to improve their social performance and their reputation with stakeholders. Nevertheless, these solutions would ever terminate the problem – i.e., resolve firms' social and environmental issues. Instead, referring to Watzlawick's description of second-order change, the one way out for corporate social and environmental issues may involve the transition from treating them as externalities to adopting them as internalities [17]. In this case social and environmental issues would no longer be con-

---

[16] Watzlawick P., Weakland J.H., Fisch R., *Change: Principles of problem formation and problem resolution*, WW Norton & Company, 2011, pp. 19-21.

[17] The concept of internalities was proposed by Porter while explaining companies

sidered as criticalities bringing trade-offs for firms' management, but as a means of transitioning to a different overall state – potentially the source of opportunities for improving firms' effectiveness and innovation while solving social and environmental problems and meeting social needs.

Applying a first-order change in the case of the firm's social dimension may contribute to the problem it is supposed to solve, as it further sharpens the contrast between the economic and social dimensions of firms' activities. Social and environmental philanthropic and responsible activities have often been introduced into the firm as a "compensation" for the negative impacts produced by firms' activities, and thus represent costs and obligations for the firms that implement them. The switch from the profit-oriented model to the CSR approach has provided dual economic-social measures that have often brought managers to consider firms' social and environmental and economic issues through a paired-antagonism perspective (such as the trade-off between economic and social performance, for example).

In this situation, problems may arise simply as the result of mistaken attempts to change critical social issues. The impression is that of the two sailors frantically steadying a (steady) boat, hanging out of their side of a sailboat in order to stabilise it, as described in Watzlawick's principles of problem formation and problem resolution: "… The more the one leans overboard, the more the other has to hang out to compensate for the instability created by the other's attempts at stabilizing the boat, while the boat itself would be quite steady if not for their acrobatic efforts at steadying it. It is not difficult to see that in order to change this absurd situation, at least one of them has to do something seemingly quite unreasonable, namely to "steady" less and not more, since this will immediately force the other to also do less of the same (unless he wants to finish up in the water), and they may eventually find themselves comfortably back inside a steady boat …" [18]. At the same way, social and economic dimension can be seen as intrinsically balanced and integrated in the strategic management processes, if the focus shifts from the trade-offs to the synergies that exist among the different patterns.

The attempt at this point of the study is to provide a critical management framework capable of allowing investigation of the dynamically changing interplay between firms' economic and social dimensions. The purpose of the management framework proposed, which considers both economic and social spheres, is to challenge this dualism by providing a

---

shared value in his different speeches held in the Shared Value Leadership Summit (2012, 2013, 2014, 2015, 2016) retrieved at www.sharedvalue.org and https://www.you tube.com/user/sharedvaluenews.

[18] Watzlawick P., Weakland J.H., Fisch R., *Change: Principles of problem formation and problem resolution*, WW Norton & Company, 2011, pp. 32-36.

two-way model that interprets the firm's activities and performance and provides a management platform for emergent adaptive social and economic party – contribution – reward patterns. Because firms are managed by people for people, the firm's activities and performance should be functionally dependent on both economic and social behaviours, related to the expectations of all the actors that contribute to the firm. If the sections of the patterns are considered and analysed separately from the whole pattern (such as, for example, the dyadic relations between parties and their contributions to the firm, or contributions evaluated on the bases of the expected returns) the risk is to lose the dynamism and the synergies between the two dimensions captured by the entire circle of exchanges that compose and define the patterns. This happens when sections of a pattern are isolated as for example in the case of the stakeholders-resources exchanges (e.g. employees-work) or shareholders-equity ones (e.g. venture capitalist-capital) and the link to the performance expectations that the parties have on firms' activities, are expressed only through the prevalent perspective offered by the traditional management models – the economic one, defining in this way only the "conventional" patterns as: employees-work-wage and venture capitalist-capital-gains. Following this approach, the patterns that are born by the connections between the two dimensions and are framed by mixed rewards, are not contemplated in the management and evaluation processes and their potential risks and opportunities in the long run will be missing. In the two examples considered, the adoption of the framework's patterns conceptualization can bring to the identification of other rewards embedded in different patterns composed by: employees-work-wellbeing or employees-work-experience in the case of stakeholders' exchange patterns and venture capitalist-capital-sustainability or venture capitalist-capital-impact in the case of shareholders' exchange patterns.

The definition of mixed rewards embedded in the cross-dimensions patterns, can be also important in the firms' process of objective setting and for the adoption of adequate measurement and communication's tools. The omission of some and/or part of the components of the patterns, can mislead the management that can put in place activities related to the economic or social targets distinctly one from another, without considering all the connections and the influences and effects they may have on the parties and resources managed by the firm. These decisions will affect also the measurement processes adopted, as they will focus on specific parts of rewards and/or resources, detecting in this way partially the needs of performance's information of the different actors involved in the firms' activities. At the same time, the performances produced in the latent patterns will not be captured and reported by the measurement processes. These "omitted" performances can emerge if the exchanges between the parties and rewards in each dimension are considered (as for example when the firm's performance is measured and reported for each category of stakeholder) but still the process will have some gaps due to the lack of the multidimensional evaluation of the resources (inputs) employed (both economic and social) and especially of the synergies that may exist between them. An example is the case when companies try to measure the benefits of a corporate child care that usually is reported as an action for the employees' wellbeing (a reward of social dimension), but rarely they quantify the effects that this action have on the employees' productivity (a resource of economic dimension). At the same way, it is difficult to figure out and measure the effects of the synergies realized by this activity in terms of being at the same time a facility for the employees and a source of efficiency for the firm. This example shows once again how the partially consideration of the patterns and their strict allocation in the two dimensions, may cause a waste of opportunities even in the cases when firms are already aware of multidimensional and mixed rewards that their processes can produce, but they still face difficulties in measuring their performance as the detection of the elements of the patterns to which they refer is not complete. As a result, part of the contributions used in the value creation process and their effects as an important part of mixed rewards, are not always fully included in the firms' performance measurement and management schemes.

Furthermore, considering only fragments of the patterns can widen the trade-off between the two dimensions as the synergies that can exist among them will be unknown to management and to the parties involved. In this way, many opportunities of shared value creation through their management, will be lost. It can be a similar representation as in the case of two opposing forces that emerge in the interaction of two entities (forces always come in pairs – equal and opposite action-reaction force pairs)[19]. If the two entities are considered separately from one-another their opposite directions or signs arise – the direction of the force on the first entity is opposite to the direction of the force on the second one. But if they are both combined within the interaction they refer to and towards the entities which they are exercised, they can "compensate" each other out, helping to achieve an equilibrium. In a similar way, our two entities, the social and economic dimensions, should be construed and analysed as part of the mutual interactions in which they are born – the firm operating in its overall system, with their attendant risks and opportunities. This can be possible if the two dimensions coexist in the management processes and are identified as the replication of the set of patterns retrieved in the firm's exchange flows specified earlier.

---

[19] The reference to the principles of the Newton's third law is reported only for illustrative purposes. No attempts of application of this principles to the framework are made.

Each dimension is represented (Figure 8) by two main categories of patterns that are developed at different levels (micro and macro) as the firms' overall system, as seen before, is made up also by structures of a higher level as market institutions (part of the economic dimension) and communities (part of the social dimension). These parties are considered in the framework as they can activate directly or indirectly important interactions with firms, influencing the individuation and the morphology of many patterns and their dynamics in time. Even though the study of these structures is not a topic of the management field, as seen previously, they find important expression in firms' both economic and social patterns as they provide important contributions for the value creation processes (through the competitive factors referring to the market institutions and cultural values related to the communities) and embodied important criteria for the setting up of the rewards and their evaluation in terms of outputs and outcomes produced by firms' activities (general welfare produced for the community; the equilibrium and efficiency of markets). As a result, the patterns made up by the elements related to market institutions and communities may influence firms' performance in many different ways and should be considered in the management processes at the same level as the ones concerning shareholders and stakeholders.

Figure 8. A theoretical framework for managing social and economic dimension patterns.

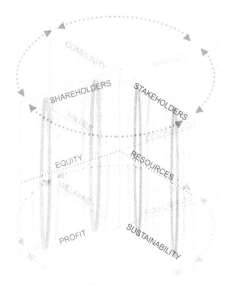

Understanding these mechanisms that determine inclusive management processes, grounded in a firm's social and economic dimension interaction patterns, provides a rationale for identifying the parties (who may be the same across different patterns and dimensions) who differentially express the ability to influence the firm's performance through their multiple contributions to the firm in return for expected multidimensional rewards from the firms' performance. Thus, there is the possibility that not only differences between patterns in the firms' social and economic dimensions but also their interaction might mediate management models and activities, influencing firms' performance. Usually, when examining firms' performance, the focus is on consolidated patterns within the economic dimension (shareholders – equity – profits), but here the framework also considers the different patterns of the social dimension and their interaction with economic ones, because they may influence and determine management processes in different ways and thus lead to different outcomes. Therefore, the measurement process adopted for management and control of the firm is established already considering extra economic resources, objectives and prerogatives embedded in the patterns that will yield results that also reflect social and environmental considerations.

Finally, the value proposition of the proposed framework is: *To provide a dynamic, synergic configuration of Parties – Contributions – Rewards patterns and the' social and economic dimensions of firms they constitute, contemplating the different phases of a firm's development, to allow the establishment of appropriate governance models, management processes and performance measurements.* This approach can guide firms in identifying strategies that are based on and fitted to their prevailing patterns, in order to support current and future decisions and establish adequate targets and measurements for their activities. In the long run, it permits the leverage of patterns that have been successful in firms' management, considering both social and economic dimensions. At the same time, attention can be paid to the "latent" patterns that represent exchanges among parties – contributions – rewards that do not belong to the same dimension but are embedded in different ones. The management of these patterns can be critical in situations when the stability of the economic and/or social dimension is threatened, as they can foster second-order change leading to a new equilibrium, by bridging the different elements and behaviours of the two dimensions through sustainable outcomes that coexist inside them.

In the next paragraphs the study will try to apply the proposed framework, focusing on the management of the firm from both economic and social perspectives, considering how the party – contribution – reward patterns related to these two dimensions can synergistically evolve and facilitate specific management processes. The implementation of the framework will also provide an explanation of how the patterns of the firm's social dimension can mediate its management activities, which can be crucial in response to novelty and to a variety of criticalities.

In order to better understand the features of the proposed framework and to test its adequacy in firms' main management needs, we examine its application in two distinct types of processes: innovation and crisis management. The choice to focus on these two topics is given by the fact that in both of them a change in the "normal" flow of the business processes occurs. In the case of innovation, the change is desirable and in a crisis context the change is required. In these two far end situations, the use and the adequacy of the framework can be better test as it has to deal with latent resources and novel competitiveness factors in the first case and mediate important change of interests and cost restriction decisions, in the second case.

2.5. Managing the social dimension for innovation

Innovation can be considered as both social and economic, outcome and process. Innovation management is an important field for studying firms' activities and performance as "... innovation contributes centrally to economic performance, corporate competitiveness, environmental sustainability, levels and nature of employment, and, in the final analysis, overall quality of life ..."[20]. If we analyse the outcome of innovation – meaning the successful application of new ideas, guided by organizational processes which achieve results through the efficient combination of various resources – it emerges that the objectives of innovation are multidimensional. In fact, the purpose of innovation is to produce positive results not only for organizations but also for their stakeholders, as it simultaneously supports growth, profit, sustainability, etc.[21] In order to achieve these variegated innovative objectives, a process of combination and coordination of complex resources, organized and implemented for innovation purposes, is needed. To identify these innovation features, the firm's innovation context is considered as the provider of innovation resources that can be grouped into the categories of people and knowledge, finance, technology, physical spaces and networks. This brief analysis reveals common ground between the characteristics of innovation and those of the proposed framework for management of the social dimension, as the latter is based on the patterns that give similar, dynamic consideration to people, their contributions and

---

[20]Dodgson M., Gann D.M., Phillips N., *The Oxford handbook of innovation management*, OUP Oxford, 2013, p. 3.

[21] *Ibidem*, p. 5.

their potential rewards, which in this case can be represented as organised for a specific target: innovation. The interactions between innovation processes and social dimension patterns become clearer if we focus on innovation management. Its purpose is to analyse how resources and capabilities are deployed and value created through the introduction of new products/services and processes underlying the set of the relations to which the innovation refers (Dodgson et al., 2013). Furthermore, the firm-based approach to innovation emphasizes the connections between context, strategy and practice, including a focus on the internal processes carried out by firms in the analysis of the innovation, as well as its outcomes and performance. As we have seen, social dimension patterns mediate the processes for managing the firm's internal and external boundaries, and are well suited to innovation management processes, which intrinsically consider these interactions. This synergy is already recognised in the field of CSR, where firms' socially responsible actions are seen as a response to the changing context of social regulation (Matten and Moon, 2008). Social dimension patterns consider further the rewards, in terms of results and impacts, that these actions can produce for the different parties involved in the business processes.

Furthermore, the principal characteristics of innovation processes, as seen through the lens of innovation management, are "… dynamic, responding to contextual change and disruption, and involve the search for and creation of variety and options; selection from within that variety from which to deliver and capture value; and propagation of successful choices creating resources and learning with which to re-invest into the cycle …"[22]. This bundle of prerogatives for innovation management are coherent with the framework for the management of the firm's social dimensions, as it can reframe existing processes, business models and value chains in response to the dynamic configuration of its different patterns.

Confirmation of the link between innovation and stakeholder management is provided by the empirical study by Ayuso et al. (2011), showing how stakeholder-regarding behaviour influences innovation. The study affirms that: "… the actively managed relationships with stakeholders can become an important source of ideas for innovations that address stakeholder expectations and ultimately contribute to the welfare of the social and natural environment. Through stakeholder engagement companies can anticipate, understand, and respond faster and more easily to changes in the rapidly changing business environment …"[23]. In framing sustainable

---

[22] *Ibidem*, p. 12.

[23] Ayuso S., Ángel Rodríguez M., García-Castro R., Ángel Ariño M., *Does stake-*

innovation, they highlight two linked "sub-capabilities": firms' ability to establish, strong, interactive relationships with stakeholders (stakeholder engagement) and their capacity to manage knowledge acquired from stakeholder (knowledge management) empirically demonstrating their impact on sustainable innovation. The study also found that the level of development of the two sub-capabilities depends on the industry: "... high knowledge intensity and high visibility towards society appear to be the most favourable conditions for developing organizational capabilities leading to sustainable innovation ..." [24]. This last result draws attention to the importance of those knowledge driven patterns of social dimension in which contributions consist of knowledge exchanged between the party that possesses it and the firm that can benefit from it. Furthermore, the rewards these parties expect from firms' activities involve a large component of trust, which requires reputation-building on the part of firms that needs to be managed.

If engaging with a firm's multiple stakeholders can affect its level of innovativeness, managing the patterns in which their resources are embedded and through which they "express" their expectancies can design opportunities for firms to develop new ways of capturing, creating and delivering innovation while managing the existing value creation processes. This consideration demonstrates that a firm's social dimension framework is of assistance in further analysing the outcomes of a multidimensional phenomenon, and can foster its management processes, as in the case of innovation.

2.5.1. Managing social innovation through the firm's social dimension

One particular type of innovation discussed separately in the innovation management literature is social innovation, characterized by the innovator's intention of transforming social arrangements (Westley and Antadze, 2010, Lawrence et al., 2011). Social innovation represents a specific set of issues that encompasses a wide range of topics in various disciplines, with different perspectives and conceptualizations (Mulgan, 2006, Phills et al., 2008, Seelos and Mair, 2012). Although this variety of studies highlights many different definitions and variables, the broad understanding of social innovation converges in its concern to solve social problems (Phills et al., 2008). In fact, the core of the study of social innovation is the relationship between how social issues are understood in order to formulate adequate, novel solutions for addressing social problems. But when attention moves

---

holder engagement promote sustainable innovation orientation?, Industrial Management and Data Systems, 111(9), 1399-1417, 2011, p. 1400.

[24] *Ibidem*, p. 1411.

further on, to the process of identifying and analysing social problems, viewpoints and studies vary (Lawrence et al., 2011). In this situation, a first step, needed for the analysis of social innovation management, is to understand that "… what constitutes a problem, its boundaries, its effects and its importance are all social negotiate phenomena that reflects the norms, values and beliefs of those involved, as well as the power relations and distributions of resources among them …" [25]. According to this position, which defines the effectiveness of innovation as the ability to identify and address social problems, it is fundamental to consider those problems as a social construction, as they are embedded in the communities that both construct the problems and act in response to these constructions. Thus, when responding to social problems through social innovation processes, companies should be aware that they are identifying only some of the social issues because these problems are socially constructed by the set of actors involved, who are directly and indirectly influenced by the process. Furthermore, considering social innovation as an embedded process of social construction focuses attention on how people can be affected *more* than on *how many* were affected by the proposed change (Lawrence et al., 2011). This attitude highlights social innovation management as a pluralistic but conflictual process, since the actors engaged in it can be inclined to maintain or disrupt the ingrained understanding of social problems. However, social innovation may occur when new solutions become a "changed common sense" (Mulgan et al., 2007). By a mechanism similar to Watzlawick's second-order change described previously, these solutions usually appear to be weird, unexpected, and uncommonsensical and provide changes in the system itself, unlike first-order change, which always appears to be based on common sense [26]. Starting with the understanding of the social problem rather than focusing on the novel solution allows the answer to be explored and can avoid "solution myopia" – an exclusive concentration on the features of the novel solution that separate it from the social context it refers to and tries to change (Lawrence et al., 2013).

The relationship between novel solutions and social problems tends to be considered as unidirectional, with the novel solution that represents an innovation univocally changing the way the social problem is comprehended and modifying the attitudes toward it. But if problems arise in a given context, they will interact with the solution using both their past behaviour

---

[25] Lawrence T.B., Dover G., Gallagher B., *Managing social innovation*, in Dodgson M., Gann D.M., Phillips N., *The Oxford handbook of innovation management*, OUP Oxford, 2014, p. 318.

[26] Watzlawick P., Weakland J.H., Fisch R., *Change: Principles of problem formation and problem resolution*, WW Norton & Company, 2011, p. 92.

and the new behaviours introduced by the change, and may thus either support or resist new solutions. In this realm, the transformation produced by social innovation is construed as a complex set of dynamic interactions between novel solutions and the existing way of thinking of social problems.

To sum up, managing social innovation involves[27]:

• understanding how social problems are constructed in a social context;
• appreciating how the construction of social problems affects potential solutions, and in turn how novel solutions might affect the ways the problems are understood, both directly and indirectly;
• analysing the complex of ideas, beliefs, values, relationships, technologies and places that connect social problems and novel solutions.

The implementation of this process of social innovation generates the need for a complex model for its management. Firms should implement suitable infrastructures and implement adequate strategies that can both focus on social problems and identify a repetitive process through which they can be linked to the creation of novel solutions. The proposed framework, which considers social dimension patterns, can be applied for this purpose as it intrinsically considers the social issues grounded in the firm's overall system, which includes the social context where the social problems are constructed, and offers a management model based on the dynamic of the patterns in relation to the community where activities are carried out and the impacts of the novel solutions are produced – the rewards expected by the community.

Another important issue related to social innovation management is the lack of practical indications for its implementation in organizations. Many reviews of the literature that consider the research on innovation applied to social projects (Crossan and Apaydin, 2010; Seelos and Mair, 2012) show that, as for innovation issues in general, the knowledge developed so far on this topic does not offer operative guidance for organizations. The absence of operative insights has brought organizations to "translate" the fragmented knowledge on social innovation into their decision-making processes themselves. This may lead them to create an "innovation language", which is intelligible to their managers and can help identify clear roles and expectations for innovation in the firms' activities in a long-term perspective (Seelos and Mair, 2017). In order to support organizations in this process,

---

[27] Lawrence T.B., Dover G., Gallagher B., *Managing social innovation*, in Dodgson M., Gann D.M., Phillips N., *The Oxford handbook of innovation management*, OUP Oxford, 2014, p. 328.

in their recent work Seelos and Mair (2017) link the evaluation of innovation-oriented processes to their potential to create impacts in terms of benefits produced for the people and communities the organizations serve. In this way, using an impact evaluation perspective for social innovation, organizations can assess its outcomes and positive impacts in relation to the social problems faced and the efforts undertaken. The linking of concrete results to concrete decisions and activities considers social innovation as "… a process that has particular characteristics, organizations, funders, and other stakeholders can reflect on innovation more systematically and learn to make better decision about it …" [28] This innovation process points to three areas where organizations must focus their attention in order to depict their impact creation approach, which may define the innovation purposes in socially-oriented firms. In particular, the authors explain why, what and how knowledge is useful for organizations when evaluating their impact-creation logic, and subdivide it into three main dimensions:

• knowledge about the nature of the problems and needs that the organization's activities refer to in a given environment;
• knowledge that accumulates as resources and capabilities considered as fundamental for offering adequate solutions. It is also the basis for evaluating the probability and features of unpredicted consequences related to the solution;
• knowledge and clarity about its core values and identity, formalized and understood in the sense of its mission. If the innovation necessitates a commitment to activities that are not in line with the organization's core values and identity, its effectiveness may be uncertain. Knowledge should be also formalized into a long-term strategy built upon concrete objectives and principles and specific managerial structures and processes [29].

In order to have a more consistent, clearer understanding of the implementation of this approach in practice, the authors have investigated these issues by analysing the social innovation archetypes in the cases of four social enterprises. The main indication that emerges from the case studies is that there are no "easy recipes", but still a clear picture of innovation as an organizational process can emerge (Seelos and Mair, 2017). Therefore, the impact-creation approach offers useful guidance on the innovation processes of production organizations and suggests different insights for their management, especially in social entrepreneurial projects.

There are many communalities between the impact-creation approach

---

[28] Seelos C., Mair J., *Innovation and scaling for impact: How effective social enterprises do it*, Stanford University Press, 2017, p. 21.
[29] *Ibidem*, pp. 22-30.

to social innovation and the social dimension framework, especially when considering the relationship between the resources needed and the organizational potential for creating impact for all the different parties. This relationship is a "fragment" of the social dimension patterns, which refers to the social dimension contributions that the firm manages and which are defined in accordance to the expected results, in which the social impact generated by the combination of these resources is embedded. Additionally, social dimension patterns consider a wider flow of exchanges, also including the parties that encompass the necessary resources and can target the innovation's impact and/or are the recipients of its outcome. The three dimensions of knowledge, proposed by the model, are embedded and can be identified in the flow of exchanges amongst the main actors in the organization's social innovation process, their understanding of social problems, and the evaluation of the resources they provide for this purpose, in relation to their impact generation expectations. Social dimension patterns extend this perspective by simultaneously considering not only the resources in relation to the results but also the perception of the parties that possess the critical resources and influence impact creation, also through their expected reward – the outcome, which the innovation process is supposed to generate.

2.6. Crisis management through the lens of the social dimension framework

A business crisis can be understood as "a specific, unexpected and non-routine event or series of events that creates high levels of uncertainty and threatens or is perceived to threaten an organization's high priority goals" [30].

This phenomenon has been identified in the last decade due to the global economic crisis that contributed to the decline and failure of many businesses, generating a loss of value not only for the single company but also for all its stakeholders and for the whole economic and social context in which the firm operated. Furthermore, during the last few years business crises have also arisen from social issues and in particular firms' environmental sphere, such as in the case of "Dieselgate", an unprecedented event not only in the car-making industry but also in the business realm in general. About 11 million cars were equipped with specially tailored devices that allowed the car to pass the emission test. The Volkswagen group lost

---

[30] Seeger M.W., Sellnow T.L., Ulmer R.R., *Communication, organization, and crisis*, Annals of the International Communication Association, 21(1), 231-276, 1998, p. 233.

its hard-earned reputation and its leading share of the diesel-powered car market. [31]

This awareness clearly indicates the need to analyse business crises from a perspective that intertwines the economic and social dimensions, and which, moreover, stems from the assumption that a firm's conventional operation and its ability to create value are based on the maintenance of a sustainable equilibrium of conditions over time. In addition, a company's inability to properly reward, through its management activities, all the productive factors employed and the expectations of its stakeholders, means that it is not operating in accordance to the principle of cost-effectiveness. Therefore, the situation of "imbalance" in which firms operate because of economic or socio/environmental crisis is prejudicial not only to the organization's economic dimension but also to the whole system of rewards for its stakeholders and the community – its social dimension.

In the management literature, the approach which includes social and environmental issues in crisis management appears in studies that apply stakeholder management to this topic (Pearson and Clair, 1998; Rowley and Moldoveanu, 2003; Alpaslan et al., 2009). As we have seen in the previous chapters, the aim of stakeholder management is to identify organizational structures, general policies and individual decisions, which have as their main concern a simultaneous attention to the interests of all the firm's stakeholders [32]. The fundamental reflection that this approach offers for the crisis management debate is the integration of the interests of various stakeholders as a necessary precondition for ensuring that institutions are able to overcome the crisis and return to long-term sustainability. The firm's social dimension framework can add additional consideration of the contribution – reward dynamic in relation to all parties potentially critical for the firm's survival to the stakeholder management approach for firms in crisis.

According to the firm social dimension management framework, decision-makers are called upon to identify the parties affected by the firm's interaction with its sub-systems and the expectations they have toward its activities. This process also determines the categories of relationships that the company establishes with these groups, based on the forms of collaboration necessary for the conduct of the company's everyday activities. Once the parties have been identified (groups for each category of parties: shareholders, stakeholders, institutions and the community) and their expecta-

---

[31] Rattalma M.F., *The Dieselgate: A Legal Perspective*, Springer, 2017.

[32] Donaldson T., Preston L., *La teoria degli stakeholder dell'impresa: concetti, evidenza ed implicazioni*, in Freeman E.R., Rusconi G., Dorigatti M., *Teoria degli stakeholder*, Franco Angeli, Milano, 2007.

tions have been mapped out, a dynamic mutual exchange process is established where both parties redefine their expectations and future behaviours, on the basis of their perception and knowledge of each other. This complex process is needed because the company's social dimension patterns may be transformed from a set of resources to a set of risks for overcoming the crisis if they are not linked to expectations in a crisis situation. At the same time, this process can help identify the opportunities embedded in the evolving "crisis patterns" of the social dimension and their interaction with the economic ones, which may enable firms to obtain the new complex of contributions needed once the rewards of the "crisis patterns" have been redefined.

In a crisis situation, where the company temporarily loses its natural regulatory mechanism (its status as a going concern, the drive towards shared goals [33]) it becomes essential to analyse its management processes, using the social dimension framework as an important mechanism not only for overcoming but also for preventing periods of crisis for the firm.

In addition, a crisis, as a complex phenomenon, is often configurable as a set of internal and external imbalances and inefficiencies, which result in economic losses and have consequences and generate stresses in the dynamics of firms' social dimension patterns.

Many studies have reported a distinction between crisis situations linked to external variables, arising from factors beyond managerial control, and those triggered by internal variables, in which the primary cause of the critical state is attributed to strategic and organizational mistakes made by the firm's management (Weick, 1998; Mitroff and Anagnos, 2001; Jacques, 2010). Variables that can represent external risks, such as industry or macroeconomic crises, are unable to cause a firm-specific crisis on their own. In fact, some studies go beyond the identification of single categories of variables, and place the complexity of the phenomenon in the centre of their analysis, as one of the major determinants of business crises. The thesis that takes an entity-based approach [34] to crises is particular relevant from this point of view. Under this approach, the phenomenon of a business crisis cannot be attributed to a single determinant factor or a negative economic trend, but must be analysed as a composite, more or less rapid process, that alters the value of an enterprise over time, due to inadequate strategic approaches and/or operational inefficiencies on the part of the company. This approach is confirmed if the social dimension framework is

---

[33] Dossena G., *Risanamento, governance e stakeholder: gestione di interessi in conflitto e conflitto di interessi*, Sinergie rivista di studi e ricerche, 71, 2011.

[34] Danovi A., Quagli A., *Gestione della crisi aziendale e dei processi di risanamento. Prevenzione e diagnosi, terapie, casi aziendali*, Ipsoa, Milano, 2008.

applied, since unfavourable external conditions are reflected in the company's social dimension patterns which, being interrelated to the company's operational characteristics and economic patterns, can generate downward trends if not managed. A crisis therefore seems to involve the simultaneous presence of several triggering factors, which reciprocally feed each other and drive the transition from economic-financial imbalance to insolvency.

This configuration of the crisis identifies a concrete need for identifying appropriate, efficient models and intervention tools for the company's management in critical conditions, in order to safeguard the expectations of all stakeholders and preserve value. As in the case of the social dimension framework, the issue of an inclusive management model and the way in which it can be handled and function during a firm crisis is, therefore, of fundamental importance.

Multidimensional analysis of business crises involves social dimension patterns, their strategic-operative dynamics and the different synergies between the firm's social and economic dimensions, in order to map out the inclusive management processes that can be implemented for firms operating in crisis contexts. Consequently, it is necessary to identify potentially more systematic crisis-oriented managerial models and enable them to move from an analytical perspective to a more operational one, capable of setting forth possible concrete actions for the firm's management. In this perspective, the application of the social dimension framework should provide rich analytical potentials and at the same time generate connotations that can meet both theoretical and operational needs simultaneously.

Since the framework for the management of the social dimension is proposed as an approach with practical implications for firms, it attempts to provide clues, recommendations and dynamic processes for applying social dimension patterns in a managerial context. It is not limited to describing existing situations or predicting cause-effect relationships, but can also be used to generate advice for firms' decision-making, by offering processes and practical guidance that jointly consider the business's social and economic behaviour. Examination of the application of this framework to specific crisis management cases reveals its main strengths to be:

• the ability to consistently manage a set of heterogeneous emerging issues. In this regard, the managerial challenge is not so much to manage the stakeholders or shareholders individually but to tackle and respond to the various resource and reward of the patterns involved in the firm's processes, which are apparently more complex from an operational point of view. The company may benefit from this complexity by coherently managing a flow of issues rather than dealing with the parties separately, losing sight of the interaction among them;

• the ability to set up a double-track crisis management process, involving both ad hoc crisis units and the various "anchor points", in the case of specific patterns more representative for both dimensions in terms of synergies between them;

• good diagnostic capabilities for detecting the firm's patterns that may represent complex criticalities, as it gives simultaneous consideration to both economic and social dimension patterns and their dynamic evolution over time;

• capability to identify "latent" patterns, fundamental for crisis management but not captured by traditional management models, since they refer to dissociated dimensions. Latent patterns may exist because of dissociated party – contributions – rewards relationships (they may be catalogued in different dimensions, not in the same one) that can influence crisis management. They may have significant relevance for crisis management, even if their single elements (party, resources, rewards) are considered not to be a top priority for the crisis process.

2.6.1. Communicating crises to stakeholders

Adopting the principles of a stakeholder approach in the context of crisis, can lead companies to figure out and implement proactive and cooperative behaviours that may be the more fruitful crisis management (Alpaslan et al., 2009). In particular: "… managers or organizations behaving more in accord with the principles of the stakeholder model aim to behave proactively or at least accommodatingly when dealing with both high salience (e.g., definitive), low salience (e.g., discretionary), and "derivatively legitimate" (e.g., dangerous) stakeholders …" [35]. Although establishing strong relationships with stakeholders is not enough to enable a company to avoid any type of crisis, good communication with them can play an important role in how the company tries to respond to a crisis that it cannot avoid.

Research on this issue suggests that management should provide clear and precise communication about the crisis to stakeholders, and as quickly as possible, even though this is a tough standard to meet (Fink, 1986, Sellnow, 1993). Many of these studies have analysed the way in which companies try to meet stakeholders' information needs after the crisis has occurred. Other stakeholder information needs may include identification of the causes of the crisis, actions taken to reduce the extent of the damage caused by the crisis, or information on how those most vulnerable to the

---

[35] Alpaslan C.M., Green S.E., Mitroff I.I., *Corporate governance in the context of crises: Towards a stakeholder theory of crisis management*, Journal of contingencies and crisis management, 17(1), 38-49, 2009, p. 43.

crisis must react to recover and move forward. Furthermore, qualitative communication should also have a positive effect on the extent to which scarce resources are developed to address the crisis promptly. Effective crises management depends on the creation of open communication channels between hierarchical levels and divisional units (Pearson and Mitroff, 1993). Studies that have analysed bidirectional symmetric communication (Grunig and Grunig, 1992; Grunig and White, 1992) show that companies actively develop mutually beneficial communication relationships with stakeholders. More specifically, members of an organization will be able to allocate scarce resources more efficiently, because they will be able to use accurate, complete information about the existence of resources and how they can be used for the optimum benefit of the entire organization.

The social dimension framework considers the two-way flow of information based on the firm's perspective toward stakeholders in the light of the resources they bring to the firm, and at the same time on stakeholders' perspective on the firm, including their expectations, as part of the patterns that are managed. The patterns that "unify" this analysis consist of the information flow which dynamically connects all those involved in it.

Another issue that emerges in crises communication concerns its contents, which are mainly dedicated to internal structures and require continuous updates, which increase the difficulty of transmitting useful information to external actors. It is important to note that most companies avoid giving explanations about the technical aspects of the crisis or limit their communication to the provision of direct factual disclaimers on these issues without offering a detailed analysis. This means that when a look at the technical details is needed, companies rarely extend the level of information provided and try to dictate the facts directly, giving little or no explanation for a wider "non-specialized" audience. All categories of stakeholders receive the same coverage of technical issues and the same type of technical explanation. On the one hand this fact can be interpreted as consistent with studies that suggest companies should send coherent messages embracing all stakeholders when communicating technical details, but on the other hand, this could be an important area of intervention for firms that adopt an inclusive approach, implementing communication strategies and giving different depths of technical explanation for the various stakeholder groups affected by the crisis. Obviously, the information content must the same, but some categories probably need more explanation than others. This may be the case where consistency actually prevails over legitimacy, in the event that the target stakeholders do not understand the technical nature of the crisis and its consequences, or when the impact that the crisis has on them is not directly linked to the technical aspects of the crisis but is rather a side-effect of these phenomena.

The risk that lies in the adoption of the same communication strategies to explain the crisis for all recipients is that some stakeholders may not fully understand their role in this process and consequently may not react proactively to the extent of the crisis. Stakeholders often need a particular type of information to make them aware of the criticalities faced and resources needed by the company in a crisis context, so that they can share and approve the necessary resources and management choices. Faced with a crisis situation, stakeholders will probably seek to deepen the information related to their position and that is why they should not be left to acquire with this information elsewhere (Augustine et al., 2000). Given these considerations, some of the abovementioned studies have analysed how companies use communication strategies in crisis contexts, trying to point out in particular whether there are differences in communication among stakeholder groups (Acquier et al., 2008; Stephens and Malone, 2010; Xu and Li, 2013). In some of the cases examined, crisis communication strategies are different depending on the stakeholder groups to which information is addressed. However, the "translation" of technical information does not change even if its target stakeholder group changes. Despite the evidence of an effective demand for more detailed technical information during a crisis, even companies which provide technical details to stakeholders do not tailor news to the recipient, accompanying it with little or no explanation. Applying the social patterns perspective to this issue, information may be addressed to the stakeholder or to the community, depending on their contribution to the crisis management process and the shortfall in rewards they are experiencing. Since this ordering of information is already part of firms' management process, it also considers the appropriate technical language, used within the pattern to which it refers. The distinction between internal and external communication tools and characteristics, is also embedded in a pattern-based management process, since the patterns' configuration considers both internal and external parties, contributions and expectations.

Chapter 3
MEASURING FIRM'S SOCIAL DIMENSION DRIVERS AND PERFORMANCE

SUMMARY: 3.1. Firm's accountability. – 3.1.1. Mandatory Non-Financial Disclosure. – 3.1.2. Non-Financial Disclosure in the European Union. – 3.2. Choosing
the right measure. – 3.2.1. The purpose of the measurement process. – 3.2.2.
The scale of the measurement process. – 3.3. Models and tools for social accounting. – 3.3.1. Value Added Statement (VAS). – 3.3.2. Costing Models (CM).
– 3.3.3. Social Return on Investment – SROI. – 3.3.4. Social Balanced Scorecard
(SBSC). – 3.3.5. Global Reporting Initiative (GRI) – Sustainability Reporting
Standards. – 3.3.6. Integrated Reporting <IR>. – 3.3.7. Auditing and assurance
of the social performance – AA1000. – 3.3.8. ISO14000. – 3.3.9. Social Accountability 8000 (SA8000). – 3.4. Social accounting process. – 3.4.1. Account
identification and data gathering. – 3.4.2. Elaboration and evaluation of the data. – 3.4.3. Reporting and auditing. – 3.4.4. Management control.

3.1. Firm's accountability

A key aspect of the social dimension patterns management process within
organizations is the measurement and disclosure of important metrics and
information[1]. The number of firms that have developed measurement
processes to analyse, drive and communicate sustainability efforts has
significantly increased in the last few years. This process has been fostered worldwide especially by the introduction of 17 Sustainable Development Goals (SDG) introduced as part of the United Nations 2030
Agenda for Sustainable Development which aim to wipe out extreme
poverty, fight inequality, and tackle climate change. More specifically, an
operative guide for companies[2], underlines five steps for companies to
maximize their contribution to the global goals: understanding the SDGs,
goals defining priorities, setting, then integrating, reporting and communicating on them.

In order for an organization to measure and report the performance of
its social dimension for the management of its patterns in its everyday activ-

---

[1] The terms "sustainability", "stakeholder", "environmental, social and governance"
(ESG), "non-financial" or "corporate social responsibility" (CSR) – accountability, disclosure and/or reporting are all used interchangeably, to describe measures and reports
with focus on firms' social dimension issues.

[2] GRI, U. WBSCDSDG compass, *The guide for business action on the SDGs*, SDG
Compass, 2015.

ities and to constantly monitor the attainment of its long term overall goals, an appropriate accounting process that individuates suitable measurement systems and performance management tools, should be put in place. Together with its provision of relevant and useful data for management decisions, the accounting information required must also enclose the qualitative attributes of accounting process in a relevant sustainability context to enable stakeholders to assess the environmental and social impact of the organization (Lamberton, 2005).

This function of accounting information is developed through the concept of accountability as "… the duty to provide an account (by no means necessarily a financial account) or reckoning of those actions for which one is held responsible. It is about identifying what one is responsible for and then providing information about that responsibility to those who have rights to that information …" [3]. In terms of accounting process, it means individuate to whom is the account made? Stakeholders are considered as possible recipient groups of the sustainability accounting information distinguishing between their contributions to an organization and their claims. The first category highlights what the information organization expects to get from its stakeholders, the latter one individuates what stakeholders need from the organization in order to provide their contribution. Considering this bidirectional flow of the information, the crucial question from a stakeholder accountability perspective has to be the engagement and "dialogue" processes they are invited to participate in (Cooper and Owen, 2007). Stakeholder accountability must consider both standpoints in order to fulfil the final goal of the accounting process.

The giving of an account is only one part of accountability framework, as this also requires that the accountee has "… the power to hold to account the person who gives the account …" [4]. Therefore, if accountability is to be achieved stakeholders need to be empowered such that they can hold the accountors to account (Cooper and Owen, 2007). This conception of accountability requires not only the provision of information, but also its value in terms of "facilitating action" [5]. In addition, the social dimension accountability that facilitate stakeholders to be part of the firm's communicative action, it must also consider the potential for new corporate envi-

---

[3] Gray R., Owen D., Adams C., *Accounting and Accountability: Social and Environmental Accounting in a Changing World*, Prentice Hall, Hemel Hempstead, 1996, p. 38.

[4] Stewart J.D., *The role of information in public accountability*, Issues in public sector accounting, 17, 13-34, 1984, p. 16.

[5] Bailey D., Harte G., Sugden R., *Corporate disclosure and the deregulation of international investment*, Accounting, Auditing and Accountability Journal, 13(2), 197-218, 2000.

ronmental and social disclosure initiatives to enter and enhance further stakeholders' accountability, in terms of facilitating their management action through adequate tools.

In this realm, the sustainability reporting is one of the most widespread tools, through which the typology of information that is communicated, allows the firms' interlocutors to evaluate the company's activities referring to its of social dimension management. This enterprise – environment communication system arises as a result of structural and coherent relations between firm's mission and corporate governance and constitutes an integral element for its management, according to a logic of coordination in which the mission makes explicit the corporate finalism; corporate governance identifies the firm's governing structure and accountability represents the company's informational aims and responsibility (Matacena and Del Baldo, 2009).

Since the social aspects are difficult to measure, as they exert some of their effects indirectly and in a long-term perspective, it is important for the firms to adopt the right tools and models that may allow stakeholders to evaluate and assess of their expectations on the firm. In fact, communication is the fundamental for the management of the patterns of social dimension and in order to enhance their role in mediating potential conflicts between social and economic issues.

As already highlighted in the previous chapters, adopting a multistakeholder perspective, the company is visualised not only through patterns of shareholders, customers and suppliers, but with a much wider range of patterns of parties related to their various contribution and expectations. The resulting exchanges through the different entities does not only affect the economic dimension: the patterns are not necessarily expressible in monetary terms but tend increasingly to convey also with values and complex resources.

The need to communicate on firms' social and ecological concerns is closely linked to the natural process of firms adapting to a changing overall system, characterized by continuous modifications, which affect the modern socio-economic landscape. The lack of confidence in economic growth without limits; the progressive sensitization of public opinion on the issues of environmental depletion and scarcity of resources in order to promote sustainable global growth; the evolution of consumption behaviours, which today are characterized by greater awareness on these topics, as they are based on a rich and articulated information substratum and on a growing consumer's negotiating power, requires a rethinking of the rules of business management around the centrality and the correct interpretation of the requests coming from all the stakeholders. Being more aware, they are in fact able to exercise, by direct and indirect way, certain pressures on social and economic issues in order to seek answers to their renewed expectations. The ability of the companies to answer to these expectations inevitably passes through the patterns of social dimension, which offers new means for pursuing the ultimate goal of corporate action – the value creation. The link between sustainable development and business activities is given by the firm social dimension that represents a reinterpretation, of the sustainability paradigm in companies' activities within decision-making, strategic and management processes, accountability (Perrini, 2006; Tencati, 2002).

What generally distinguishes social accountability from the traditional economic accountability is the requirement of a level of voluntariness: the economic entity that wants to stand out in order to be socially responsible, does so by spontaneously and proactively aligning its management strategy with the pursuit of higher social and ethical standards, which go beyond the constraints of the law. Therefore, it is not a question of limiting itself to the fulfilment of legal requirements but, more broadly, of constructing a proactive and active corporate identity, which is detected within the set of patterns of firm social dimension. Moreover, the voluntary assumption of social and environmental communication, is reflected in the setting of official documents published by the main communication standard setters: these documents offer useful guidelines and food for thought, in the knowledge that the complexity of the phenomenon is such that each firm must freely make the adaptations ascribable to the specificity of the case (while recognizing the importance of ensuring a certain level of uniformity). In general, one the most widespread form of social accountability – the sustainability reporting, which summarizes the economic, social and environmental performances of the company, is a direct expression of the willingness to communicate, measuring the firm social dimension.

On the importance of social accountability, the opinion of economic operators has reached a point of cohesion that suggests that we are facing a phenomenon that is now triggered with a certain stability and such as to arouse interest in industrial associations, academic circles and individual companies. In fact, social accountability is a common issue for the private sector as well as for the public sector and has produced in recent years a critical mass of consensus functional to the continuation and further development of this phenomenon.

However, the proliferation of accountability documents in the firms' context, in some cases similar in content but with different denominations or similar in the denomination but different in content, has given rise to the need for a certain level of standardization, in order to facilitate comparability of the documents and therefore the performance they report, considering their allocation in time and in space. At an international level the UN and OECD recommendations have been a starting point for a global harmonization and for several research groups have tried to cope with this need by elaborating in turn a series of guidelines for the construction of social reporting documents. Summing up, the various approaches proposed by the international organizations (UN Global Compact, Global Reporting Initiative, International Integrated Reported Council, etc.) can be considered the principle paths followed by organizations in the construction of the document that can be traced back to a standard that is process-oriented and/or to a standard content-oriented. In the first case, the guidelines leverage the actions that guide the construction of a report whose purpose is to periodically monitor the performance in terms of sustainability (see the contribution of the AA1000 and GRI standards). The documents developed on the basis of content standards, on the other hand, have the objective of providing guidelines with particular regard to the structure and content of the document. In both cases the guidelines on which the company decides to build its reporting process and define the document forms (CSR Reports, Sustainability Reports, Mission Reports, Social Reports, etc.), emphasizing the importance of a common denominator that helps the process of an effective integration of firms economic and social dimension and its communication in firm's overall system.

More precisely, the sustainability reporting allows companies to carry out an overall assessment of their performance, in quantitative and qualitative terms. The quantitative contribution is made up not only of the costs and revenues of the Income Statement and of the assets and liabilities of the Balance Sheet, but also of all the positive and negative externalities that the firm's activities produce. By shifting the evaluation plan to a more global level, the document does not only express management in terms of cost-benefit analysis, but in terms of quality, expressed in terms of the ethical values that the company assumes and respect in its activities. All the reporting processes can support the decisional and planning processes, aimed at increasing the degree of consent and legitimacy among the various social dimension actors.

Therefore, the proliferation of norms, recommendations and practices by international institutions has taken place, trying to eliminate conflicts of interest, so that the communicative transparency induced re-establishes external trust and the systematic nature of information will bring reputational benefits to firms in its overall system. Even though it is difficult to talk about a possible unitary and systematic integrated communication. Although the economic accountability of all companies on the market is equal and regulated by the normative, their social and environmental accountability is different, because the mission and the corporate governance are different in each type of company (Matacena, 2009). This is also consistent with the conceptualisation of the firm's social and economic dimension and their patterns' management which validate the importance of exchange of information between firms and their stakeholders, both qualitative and quantitative.

In particular, considering the different configurations of the patterns of firm social and economic dimension, social accountability may concern various levels of information needs:

– in profit organizations, it is connected to the maintenance of conditions of legitimacy and consent, subtended by the finalism of social and economic sustainability;

– in non-profit organizations, it is rooted in their mutualism purpose, and can be retrieved in the coherence between their activities' outcomes and their mission and governance;

– in social enterprises, is represented by the social purpose pursued and the related impact produced.

In order to fit to all of these distinctive issues, the social accountability process should be grounded in the configuration of the patterns of the social dimension of the firm considering at the same time its interaction with the economic one. As a result, an effective stakeholder accountability passes through a process of accounting that fits and is part of the patterns' management practices.

In the next sessions, the main models and instruments that refer to social accountability will be reported trying to highlight their main features and their ability to answer to different firms' accountability issues. Grounded on these characteristics, a process of social accounting for measuring and managing firm's social dimension performance, will be provided and analysed.

3.1.1. Mandatory Non-Financial Disclosure

As a direct consequence of the increasing demand of companies' social accountability, many countries around the world have begun to mandate the disclosure of social and environmental information, either through specific laws and regulations or through stock exchange listing requirements. Aa a result, there has been a proliferation of regulations aiming to incentivize companies, all over the world, to improve their environmental, social and governance (ESG) accountability. The rise of "comply or explain" approaches in many areas of the world and the increasing activity of financial market regulators and stock exchanges, has contribute to further develop the social accountability processes, models and instruments. European countries are leading this process in terms of both regulatory and operational instruments applied[6]. In fact, many new instruments were put in place by EU member states in the process of national implementation measures, relate to the transposition of a specific EU Directive on Non-Financial Reporting. The EU Commission required reporting not only on specific environmental or social issues but also more widely on non-financial performance.

In the USA, the SEC (Securities Exchange Commission) has traditionally applied to ESG reporting, a framework that was established in the 1970s, in response to rulemaking petitions and litigation seeking to compel the Commission to adopt environmental and equal employment disclosure requirements. Afterward, in 2010 the SEC has issued a guidance document relating to climate change issues in its "Climate Change Guidance" in which it describes several disclosure requirements which potentially may relate to climate change[7].

Recently, for reviewing and updating the sustainability disclosure, the SEC issued a "Concept Release" seeking public comments on 340 topics relating to business and financial disclosure requirements for publicly-traded companies[8].

In Latin America, non-financial reporting also grew quickly with a significant number of instruments issued by governments and financial regulators. In particular, countries with mandatory disclosure on non-financial information are: Argentina, Brazil, Colombia, Costa Rica, Mexico, Peru and Chile[9].

Asia Pacific has shown strong growth of sustainability reporting regulations too. Many of the accountability instruments are provided in the reporting rules introduced by financial market regulators. In particular, in many countries, stock exchanges and financial or industry regulators are now adding new drivers to the mandatory reporting instruments. In the past, the main requirements and instruments were provided by governments. This incremental trend in many Asian countries including India, In-

---

[6] KPMG, GRI, UNEP CCGA, *Carrots and Sticks: Global Trends in sustainability reporting regulation and policy*, KPMG Advisory NV, Global Reporting Initiative, Centre for Corporate Governance in Africa, United Nations Environment Programme, 2016.

[7] SEC Guidance Regarding Disclosures Related to Climate Change, *Climate Change Guidance*, 8/02/2010.

[8] For further information, refer to SEC "Concept Release", 81 Fed. Reg. 23916, 22/04/2016.

[9] Boje D.M., *Organizational change and global standardization: Solutions to standards and norms overwhelming organizations*, Routledge, 2015.

donesia, Malaysia and South Korea, is confirmed by high rates of sustainability disclosure driven by regulation [10].

3.1.2. Non-Financial Disclosure in the European Union

The growing importance of the social and environmental measurement and
reporting in Europe is confirmed and followed by specific legislation
adopted by the European Union Member States on disclosure of non-
financial and diversity information [11].

The source of these regulation is the Directive 2014/95/EU of the European Parliament and of the Council of 22 October 2014 that aims to improve and harmonise the disclosure of non-financial information. Its objective is to help organizations fulfil the requirement to disclose relevant and
useful information on environmental and social issues in a reliable and
more comparable way. Such disclosure obligations are set out in the Directive on disclosure of non-financial and diversity information and are
mandatory for all large companies and public-interest entities. More precisely, the Directive 2014/95/EU states that "large companies" – those having an average number of employees in excess of 500, and "public-interest
entities" – listed companies, credit institutions, insurance undertakings,
and others defined by Member States as public-interest entities, should
prepare a non-financial statement with information on environmental, social, employee-related, anti-corruption and bribery matters, respect for
human rights, and diversity issues. The Directive affirms that: "… the disclosure of non-financial information is vital for managing change towards
a sustainable global economy by combining long-term profitability with
social justice and environmental protection …" [12]. In this context, disclosing non-financial information can foster the processes of measuring, managing and monitoring companies' performance and their impact on the
society.

---

[10] KPMG, GRI, UNEP CCGA*Carrots and Sticks: Global Trends in sustainability reporting regulation and policy*, KPMG Advisory NV, Global Reporting Initiative, Centre
for Corporate Governance in Africa, United Nations Environment Programme, 2016.

[11] For a complete overview of how Member States have implemented the Directive
2014/95/EU refer to: CSR Europe, Global Reporting Initiative (GRI), *Member State
Implementation of Directive 2014/95/EU, A comprehensive overview of how Member
States are implementing the EU Directive on Non-financial and Diversity Information*,
2017, accessed on 27 September 2017 at: https://www.csreurope.org/sites/default/files/
uploads/CSR%20Europe_GRI%20NFR%20publication_0.pdf.

[12] Directive 2014/95/EU of the European Parliament and of the Council of 22 October 2014, p. 1.

There are three levels of disclosures provided by the Directive:

– at a general level (Article 19), the disclosures cover the undertaking's business model. Its explanation for not having a relevant sustainability policy or for not disclosing certain information; and its use of external assurance;

– a second level concerns the diversity disclosure (Article 20), demanding a description of organization's diversity policy in relation to its administrative, management and supervisory bodies. If the organization does not have a relevant diversity policy, it should explain why.

Finally, the disclosure on sustainability topics (Article 19, and in the Directive's Recital) individuates information to be reported for the following categories [13]:

1. Environmental matters;
2. Social matters;
3. Employee matters;
4. Human Rights matters;
5. Anti-corruption and bribery matters.

For each of these five sustainability matters, the required disclosures take the same, two-part form:

- information points for each sustainability matter described in the following points:
    - a description of the policy pursued by the undertaking in relation to those matters, including due diligence processes implemented;
    - the outcome of those policies;
    - the principal risks related to those matters linked;
    - to the undertaking's operations including, where relevant and proportionate, its business relationships, products or services which are likely to cause adverse impacts in those areas, and how the undertaking manages those risks;
    - non-financial key performance indicators relevant to the particular business.
- specifications from the Directive's Recital request more specific, detailed disclosures about each sustainability matter.

The disclosure is also expected to include "information on the due dili-

---

[13] Directive 2014/95/EU of the European Parliament and of the Council of 22 October 2014, Art. 19, Amendments to Directive 2013/34/EU, Article 19a, Non-financial statement.

gence processes implemented by the undertaking, also regarding, where relevant and proportionate, its supply and subcontracting chains ..." [14]. This requirement clearly explicates that also the disclosure on of the supply chain or value chain is required – not just a focus on the undertaking of direct ownership or control.

This normative opens a new era for the accounting and reporting of social and environmental issues of firms as it requires not only ex-post results to be communicated but also an ex-ante planning and managing of the social and environmental performance integrated in the companies' strategy. This means that companies that are producing this information for the first time should think about it as the result of a process implemented in the strategic management assessment, through the entire supply chain of the companies and included in the management practices.

New issues emerge also for the auditing process of the companies, as the social and environmental data enter to be part of the institutional documents for which the law requires an external audit and verification.

3.2. Choosing the right measure

Comparison of the various models of firms' social and environmental impact measurement and identification of their main distinguishing features at the operating level (Bagnoli and Megali, 2011; Nicholls, 2009; Swanson and Di Zhang, 2010) has brought considerable steps forward in terms of both their validation and their use. However, one noticeable gap is the lack of theoretical foundations for the comparison between the various models (Kroeger and Weber 2014). Theoretical studies which set out to understand and analyse the creation of value in the social context have occasionally been preceded by analyses of their use, first addressing the problem of measurement (Reinhartd 2011; White 2010). If the model used for measuring a multidimensional performance is analysed without first investigating its individual sources, the risk is that the same measure may be used to assess dimensions which are actually of different kinds. It is therefore fundamental to start by choosing the approach adopted, while never forgetting the parameter to be measured – the social and environmental impact to be assessed in the firms' management processes. All the models address important management issues, but their aim is mainly to demonstrate firm's results in managing its social dimension without analysing the influence that these results have in the economic dimension and their consequences in its main patterns.

---

[14] Directive 2014/95/EU of the European Parliament and of the Council of 22 October 2014, Art. 6, p. 2.

Considering these criticalities and the intrinsic characteristics which measurement processes must provide for the firms' management (objectivity, comparability, etc.), in this chapter the models for identifying, measuring, monitoring and reporting firm's social dimension will be analysed with the aim to figure out a social accounting process that considers patterns of both social and economic dimension. This decision arises from the fact that studies in the field of social accounting have already reached maturity in tackling the problem of the measurement of resources and the multidimensional interests of the various stakeholders through the concepts and mechanisms used in accounting itself (Mook et al. 2007; Bengo et al. 2015). However, firms should be aware that the impact produced by the patterns of the social dimension, cannot be considered in separation from the overall value generated by the economic dimension, but must rather be integrated within it. After all, social and environmental performance without its economic component is a partial result, completely lacking of the assessment of its sustainability and its potential for replication and scaling over the long term. The social accounting approach can be best suited for identifying and evaluating also the results generated by the synergies among patterns of social and economic dimension.

Social accounting is based on the combination of the various stakeholders' needs for information and the balancing of their respective social and economic interest and expectations, which may often be conflicting (Gray 2002; Mathews 2004; Lamberton 2005). This is an important feature for measuring the performance in the patterns of social dimension which are based on exchanges addressed by a complex system of stakeholders. Moreover, the relationships between the various patterns composing the social dimension are on a variety of levels (institutional, social, economic and cultural, etc.) and evolve over time, since the firm's overall system is constantly changing.

Therefore, the social accounting process could be tailored more closely to the specific characteristics of the patterns of social dimension, since it offers a measurement process based on an analysis of interests and expectations of various kinds with the aim of achieving a higher level of accountability. Moreover, like its traditional equivalent, social accounting is required to fulfil a multiplicity of informative functions within the company's processes (Cooper and Owen 2007; Unerman and Bennett 2004).

In this realm, the question that the analysis attempts to answer is: which are the main features of the models based on social accounting measurement in assessing and internally and externally communicating multidimensional results, in relation to the main needs of social dimension patterns? Afterward, the main characteristics individuated by the analysis, are used for setting up a classification of the main models reported in Table 2.

3.2.1. The purpose of the measurement process

As mentioned before, the reporting functions assigned to the accounting system are expressed in the concept of accountability, meaning the obligation to provide the reader with a specific type of information and allow the assessment of actions related to an area of responsibility, performance with regard to which must be evaluated. Typically, these reporting obligations are established by regulations or legislation and verified by the institutions assigned to monitor them. Social and environmental reporting is considered as discretionary for traditional enterprises, but it assumes a role of primary importance when it becomes an essential prerequisite in the cases it must comply with the criteria established by the regulatory framework.

What is required is therefore to identify what the enterprise is responsible for and provide information about its operations to the parties which need to receive this information in order to monitor its performance (Gray, Owen, and Adams 1996). Given this two-way flow in information, the measurement model chosen must be capable of translating the "dialogue" between the stakeholders on the one hand and the enterprise on the other into a language meaningful for the assessment of value (Cooper and Owen 2007). Furthermore, according to the concept of patterns that constitute firm's social dimension, the various exchanges, in the broad sense, must consider potential sender and recipient groups of accounting information, and can be classified on the basis of their inputs to the organisation and their expectations in terms of returns. This process must contemplate both points of view and information flows direction simultaneously, in order to satisfy the final objective of the social impact measurement process, that of assessing how and to what extent the firm social dimension in accordance with the economic one is pursuing its mission, considering the use of all type of resources.

Another important reporting requirement, often necessary for the assessment of social and environmental impact of products and/or processes, is the evaluation of the processes' performance in terms of long-term sustainability (Epstein, 2008).

Social impact is created in processes which innovate social products or services with the final aim of innovation of the system itself. In order to take effect, this process must include changes in concepts and mentalities which are sustainable over the long term and capable of spontaneously taking effect in different contexts and situations. According to the Open Book of social innovation (Murray et al. 2010) this is normally reflected in all four sectors: the economy, government, society and the family. This also implies the need for modifications to the main measurement models used to quantify and manage the change taking place.

3.2.2. The scale of the measurement process

As well as fulfilling a reporting function for a variety of players, in traditional accounting the results of the measurement processes can be used for
planning and control processes, to bring behaviours into line with the
company's overall objectives (Cerbioni et al. 2011). The standard distinction is between analytical accounting – with outputs addressed mainly to
recipients within the company – and general accounting, intended mainly
for external players. This distinction also bears in mind the different main
objectives of these two accounting categories: on the one hand, general accounting is used primarily for measuring assets and liabilities and establishing the overall result for a period, while on the other, analytical accounting
is used to calculate specific results, such as the costs of products and processes, margins on various areas of business, etc. (Garrison et al. 2003). On
the basis of the various underlying aims of accounting processes, the aim is
to provide an initial analysis of issues which can be served by the different
social dimension measurement models: (internal and/or external use and
measurement of specific and/or overall results). The prevalent approach in
traditional accounting involves the identification, acquisition, measurement
and analysis of financial data in order to support companies' decision-
making process (IASB, 2010). Accounting is therefore the shared "language" used for economic and financial information about the company's
business, used to inform stakeholders, both external (shareholders, creditors, etc.) and internal (owners and managers), or institutions and regulatory bodies (such as tax authorities and stock exchanges, etc.) how the company is pursuing its economic and overall returns in the short and long run.
This information is usually supplied by means of formal documents such as
financial statements, sustainability reports, business plans, industrial plans,
etc., which provide quantitative and qualitative explanations of how resources are managed within the firm's operations and report the results
achieved.

Social impact measurement involves a number of complex, widely differing dialogues which must be made intelligible for the parties which need
to interpret them. Therefore, the recipients of "internal" strategic information are the patterns that involve the parties to whom the process of creating the social impact is mainly addressed, and those responsible for the
management of the firm's operations. "External" information is intended
the patterns of social dimension in the broader sense, including institutions, society, the environment, etc.

3.3. Models and tools for social accounting

Although it is difficult to precisely measure social performance, both academics and practitioners have developed economic, and financial analysis techniques that provide reasonable estimates for social and environmental performance measurement and communication.

To the different theoretical studies on the topic, correspond a number of organization that have begun to adopt advanced social and environmental accounting methodologies. Many initiatives offer organizations tools and guidance for developing their sustainability strategy and reporting. At the same time, there have been various attempts to classify the many measurement models created over the years (Bengo et al. 2015; Maas and Liket 2011; Nicholls 2005; Nicholls 2015). In the next paragraphs, an analysis of the main features of the most cited and widely adopted models [15] will be briefly described and analysed considering their main characteristics in terms of purpose of measurement they may potentially serve and considering their use in internal/external communication of the overall/partial performance measurement as shown in Table 1.

Table 1. Social dimension measurement main features.

The purpose of the measurement	The scale of the measurement process			
	Communication		Results	
	Internal	*External*	*Specific*	*Overall*
Regulation/Compliance				
Sustainability				
Values/Mission				
Welfare/Social Impact				

3.3.1. Value Added Statement (VAS)

The Value Added Statement was conceptualized for the first time in the study of Suojanen (1954). He suggested the Value Added Statement as a

---

[15] The analysed models were selected from those proposed in Bengo I., Arena M., Azzone G., Calderini M., *Indicators and metrics for social business: a review of current approaches*, Journal of Social Entrepreneurship, 7(1), 1-24, 2015. They analyse seventy-six models from academic and operating databases by means of keywords and then subdivided them into four clusters on the basis of their main characteristics: quantitative, holistic, qualitative and managerial. Using Scopus citations, one of the most important databases of abstracts and quotations from the peer-reviewed literature, the most cited models for each category were selected.

supplemental report, which analyses "… the value added in production and its source or distribution among the organization participants …" [16]. He suggested the value added concept for income measurement, as a way for management to fulfil their accounting duty to the various interest groups by providing more information than was possible from the income statement and balance sheet.

The value added can be defined as the value created by the organization carrying out its activities and managing the contribution of its employees as for example in the case of a manufacturing company calculating the difference of the sales less the cost of bought goods and services used in the production processes. The value added statement (VAS) reports on the calculation of value added and its application among the stakeholders in an organization. The information included in the VAS is the same to the one already contained in the income statement – salaries and wages used to be the only additional information, but it presents the information in a different and more comprehensible format. The value added statement representation is shown in Figure 9.

Figure 9. Value Added representation.

Revenues
Market Value
of outputs

External
Inputs
Goods and
Services

Value Added
- Employees
- Shareholders
- Government
- Local Communities

In contrast to profit, which is the wealth created only for the owners or shareholders, value added represents the wealth created for several groups of stakeholders (Burchell, Clubb, and Hopwood 1985; Riahi-Belkaoui, 1999). This characteristic makes the value added statement a broader scheme, focused on the wider implications of an organization's activities beyond its profits or losses (Meek and Gray, 1988).

The organization carrying out its productive activities rewards investors and creditors for risking their capital but at the same time employs people, contributes to societal costs paying taxes, and contributes to the community. If it stops to exist, the shareholders will lose the possibility to gain profits from their capital but also employees will lose their job and in general

---

[16] Suojanen W.W., *Accounting theory and the large corporation*, Accounting Review, 391-398, 1954, p. 396.

the community in which organization operates will lose "the value" it leaves within it.

To illustrate how the value added calculation process is performed, consider a manufacturing company producing muffins. The value added is calculated by taking the difference between the price the muffins are sold for and the cost of the materials that went into making the muffins (flour, sugar, eggs, electricity used, etc.). Suppose that a box of muffins is sold on average for 5 € and 100 boxes were sold, and the flour and materials cost per unit is 4 €, the value added would be 500 € minus 400 €, or 100 €. Value added can be consider as the incremental value that through labour and capital is given to the raw materials transforming them into a new form. In our example the manufacturing activity, elaborating the inputs into the final product, increments the initial value of the materials by 100 €. That value added, 100€, is then distributed to the stakeholders of the company – its employees, creditors, government (paying taxes), and shareholders.

The Value Added Statement defines value in a much broader way than profit for shareholders, and uses a stakeholder approach in its reporting. One of the limitations of the traditional value added statement is that it focuses only on financial items and pays no attention to intangibles and items that do not pass through the market and it does not account for indirect impacts of an organization's activities (Staden and Vorster, 1998).

A version of the value added statement is the Expanded Value added Statement (EVAS) that addresses some of the difficulties in applying accounting models developed for business enterprises to non-profit organizations (Mook et al., 2007). Their efficiency and effectiveness cannot be determined through information in financial statements only as they receive funds from sponsors who do not expect monetary benefits in return (Razek et al., 2000). By combining financial and social value added, the EVAS highlights the link and interdependence of the economy, community and environment (Mook et al., 2007). In general, EVAS contain two parts: the calculation of value added by an organization and its distribution to the stakeholders.

3.3.2. Costing Models (CM)

Many studies have tried to develop approaches for estimating and measuring the costs of the social and environmental impacts of organisations' activities. Bebbington and Gray (1993) state that sustainable cost can be defined as the amount that an organisation must spend to put the environmental resources at the end of the accounting period back into the original state (or at least at its equivalent) it was in at the beginning of the accounting period. This estimation would be considered as a notional one, and disclosed as a measure to the firms' profit and loss account. These concepts have been developed into different models of social accounting such as the Full cost accounting, Life-cycle assessment and Natural capital inventory accounting.

– Full cost accounting allocates all direct and indirect costs to a product or product line for inventory valuation, profitability analysis, and pricing decisions. Full cost accounting as with Mathews' total impact accounting (Mathews, 1993; 2004), attempts to capture the total costs resulting from an organisation's economic activities, including social and environmental costs (Deegan and Newson, 1996), attempting to value these impacts in financial terms.

– Life-cycle assessment is a design discipline used to minimize the environmental impacts of products, technologies, materials, processes, industrial systems, activities, and services. (Klöpffer, 2003). Life-cycle cost has been defined as the amortized annual cost of a product, including capital costs, and disposal costs discounted over the lifetime of a product.

– Natural capital inventory accounting involves the recording of stocks of natural capital over time, with changes in stock levels used as an indicator of the (declining) quality of the natural environment. Various types of natural capital stocks are distinguished enabling the recording, monitoring and reporting of depletions or enhancements within distinct categories (Gray, 1994).

3.3.3. Social Return on Investment – SROI

Social Return on Investment (SROI) is a framework for measuring and reporting a much broader concept of value; it seeks to reduce inequality and environmental degradation and improve wellbeing by incorporating social, environmental and economic costs and benefits (Nicholls et al., 2012).

SROI measures change in ways that are relevant to the people or organisations that experience or contribute to it [17]. It captures the ex post situation compared with the ex-ante one by measuring social, environmental and economic outcomes using monetary values to represent them. As a result, a ratio of benefits to costs is calculated. This ratio shows the value of the social and environmental impact that has been created in financial terms and that's why the calculation of SROI and a more precise analysis is usually provided for the evaluation of the social impact investments. In fact, the main use of SROI is made in financial terms as it helps to evaluate social benefit against the cost of investment.

---

[17] Arvidson M., Lyon F., McKay S., Moro D., *Valuing the social? The nature and controversies of measuring social return on investment (SROI)*, Voluntary Sector Review, 4(1), 3-18, 2013, p. 3.

In terms of accounting process, SROI represents a framework for evaluating the value created as a result of the calculation of the costs of the related intervention performed and the benefits it has produced in financial terms. Through the SROI measurement process firms may figure out how value is created in the patterns of its social dimension and this is just as important as what the ratio expressions.

In particular, the SROI model outlines a methodology for calculating value as well as prescribing a set of principles for the framework[18]. The seven principles are:

• Involve stakeholders;
• Understand what changes;
• Value the things that matter;
• Only include what is material;
• Do not over-claim;
• Be transparent;
• Verify the result.

The approach is focused on attributing financial value to inputs and outcomes, leading to the process of calculating the SROI ratio. In order to estimate the positive (or negative) social value of non-traded, non-market goods, the SROI model uses financial proxies. The outcome, that is, the value created, should be related to the investments made, and is expressed through a ratio that is its distinctive feature. SROI measurement should be matched by qualitative evidence based on stakeholder demands and expectations of the activity being analysed (Nicholls et al, 2009).

SROI aims to both measure and communicate internally and externally as it provides the basis for forecasting, planning and managing social oriented activities and for combined evaluation of the impact of an intervention (Wright et al, 2009). It emphasises that it provides a framework for a systematic assessment of achievements (Nicholls et al, 2009). Thus, it can bridge the gap in social dimension measurement and communication that derives from weaknesses found in other tools.

3.3.4. Social Balanced Scorecard (SBSC)

The concept of the Balanced Scorecard was developed trying to figure out which are the drivers and determinants of firms' competitive advantages beyond the financial capital. It considers "soft" factors such as knowledge, intellectual capital, customer orientation, etc., that influence the firms' per-

---

[18] Nicholls J., Lawlor E., Neitzert E., Goodspeed T., *A guide to social return on investment*, Lothian, The SROI Network, 2012, p. 9.

formance. Kaplan and Norton suggested this new performance measurement approach – the Balanced Scorecard (BSC) centred on corporate strategy considering its four main perspectives (Kaplan and Norton, 1992, 1996, 2001). The BSC aims to measure the contribution and the transformation of "soft" factors and intangible assets into long-term financial success and thus controllable (Figge et al., 2002). The BSC's four perspectives are described and represent by Kaplan and Norton as follows [19]:

1. The financial perspective indicates whether the transformation of a strategy leads to improved economic success;
2. The customer perspective represents the means through which firms tries to achieve competitive advantage in customer/market segments in which the business competes;
3. The internal process perspective includes those internal processes of firms' activities that are oriented to meet the expectations mainly of customers and shareholders;
4. Finally, the learning and growth perspective describes the framework required for the achievement of the objectives of the other three perspectives (as employees' qualification, motivation, information systems, etc.).

The purpose of BSC is to provide a prioritization and pinpoint the existing link among the strategic objectives detected and measured in the four perspectives, considering the firm's strategy and applying a financial perspective orientation. The indicators that are the measures formulated in each perspective, are basically categorized in lagging and leading indicators (Kaplan and Norton, 1996). Lagging indicators and long-term strategic objectives are formulated for the strategic core issues of each perspective derived from the strategy of the firm and show if the strategic objectives (the expected results) in each perspective were achieved. The leading indicators capture the specific drivers (that are firm specific) of the competitive advantage of the firms, explaining how the results measured by the lagging indicators, should be reached.

The balanced scorecard (BSC) is an instrument for performance measurement but not only. In order to bridge the gap between strategic and operative planning, it was further developed beyond its original conception into a strategic management concept used to communicate and coordinate the translation of the business strategy (Kaplan and Norton, 1996). In particular, Kaplan and Norton subdivide the strategic management system of the BSC into four partial processes that aim to the long-term achievement

[19] Figge F., Hahn T., Schaltegger S., and Wagner M., *The sustainability balanced scorecard–linking sustainability management to business strategy*, Business strategy and the Environment, 11(5), 269-284, 2002.

of the strategic objectives. Furthermore, Kaplan (Kaplan and Norton 2001), Somers (2005), and Bull (2007) move from the original Kaplan and Norton's balanced scorecard trying to incorporate the consideration of different groups of stakeholders, for tailoring the above model to the specificities of social perspective.

Conceptually, management of environmental and social aspects with the BSC seeks to address the problem of corporate contributions to sustainability in an integrative way. It suggests that for companies to contribute to sustainable development, it is desirable that corporate performance improves in all three dimensions of sustainability – economic, environmental and social – simultaneously (Figge et al., 2001). This means that it can be applied to integrating environmental and social issues into the successful implementation of both corporate strategies and explicit corporate social strategies.

There are basically three possibilities to integrate environmental and social aspects in the BSC. First, environmental and social aspects can be integrated in the existing four standard perspectives. Second, an additional perspective can be added to take environmental and social aspects into account. Third, a specific environmental and/or social scorecard can be formulated (Epstein, 1996; Figge et al., 2001).

The Balanced Scorecard can help organizations strategically manage patterns of social and economic dimensions as it aligns the cause-and-effect relationships of external market forces and impacts with internal social and economic drivers, values and behaviours. It is this alignment combined with social reporting that can enable firms to implement either broad differentiation or innovation strategies.

3.3.5. Global Reporting Initiative (GRI) – Sustainability Reporting Standards

Among the international reporting standards, Global Reporting Initiative (GRI) Standards, a process-oriented model with a particular focus on the document, are the world' most widely used sustainability reporting framework.

The last version of GRI Sustainability Reporting Standards published in October 2016 and effective for reports or other materials published on or after 1 July 2018, are the *GRI Standards* composed by *Universal Standards 100 series* and *Topic-specific Standards 200, 300, 400 series*.

In particular, the Universal Standards 100 series enclosed three main documents:

– GRI 101: The foundation that is the starting point for using the set of GRI Standards. GRI 101 sets out the Reporting Principles for defining report content and quality. It includes requirements for preparing a sustainability report in accordance with the GRI Standards, and describes how the GRI Standards can be used and referenced. GRI 101 also includes the specific claims that are required for organizations preparing a sustainability report in accordance with the Standards, and for those using selected GRI Standards to report specific information.

– GRI 102: General Disclosures is used to report contextual information about an organization and its sustainability reporting practices. This includes information about an organization's profile, strategy, ethics and integrity, governance, stakeholder engagement practices, and reporting process.

– GRI 103: Management Approach is used to report information about how an organization manages a material topic. It is designed to be used for each material topic in a sustainability report, including those covered by the topic – specific GRI Standards (series 200, 300, and 400) and other topics that are consider material.

The topic-specific Standards are used to report information on an organization's impacts related to economic, environmental, and social issues and includes 200 series on economic topics, the 300 series on environmental topics and the 400 series on social topics.

In the GRI Standards, the term of sustainability reporting is considered synonymous with others used to define reporting on economic, environmental, and social impacts (e.g., triple bottom line report, corporate responsibility reporting, etc.).

In order to guarantee the quality of the measurements, the GRI reporting principles individuate the criteria that sustainability reports must follow in order to give a truthful view of the economic, social and environmental status of the reporting organization. Using the same principles can increase the timely comparability between organizations situated in different geographical areas and over time. The compliance to the GRI reporting principles are the starting point for the process of reporting, determine the content and presentation of the reporting, and ensure quality and reliability of the information reported. Reporting Principles are subdivided in two groups one where are included the principles defining the content and the other contains principles for defining the quality of reporting. The first group is composed by principles that that deal with the question what to report, already analysed in the first phase of the accounting process analysed (stakeholder inclusiveness, materiality, completeness and sustainability context). Reporting Principles define the outcomes a report should achieve and guide decisions throughout the reporting process and how to report on selected topics and indicators in order to help achieve data transparency. "... The quality of information is important for enabling stakeholders to make sound and reasonable assessments of an organization, and to take appropriate actions ..." [20]. In fact, stakeholders are at the centre of the setting of GRI reporting process, being the protagonists of the principles for the definition of the report content:

1. Stakeholder Inclusiveness – the organization shall identify its stakeholders, and explain how it has responded to their reasonable expectations and interests.

2. Sustainability Context – information on performance should be placed in the organization's context of sustainability, reporting how an organization contributes, or aims to contribute, to the improvement or deterioration of economic, environmental, and social conditions at the local, regional, or global level.

3. Materiality – the data reported should cover relevant topics defined as those that can reasonably be considered important according to the organization's economic, environmental, and social impacts, or that influence the decisions of stakeholders.

4. Completeness – the report shall include the topics that have pass the materiality test and assure that their Boundaries are sufficient to reflect significant economic, environmental, and social impacts, and to enable stakeholders to assess the reporting organization's performance in the reporting period.

The section containing principles that guide choices on ensuring the quality of reported information, includes decisions related to the process of preparing information for the report. Balance, comparability, accuracy, timeliness, clarity and reliability principles cover the quality of the reported information.

The report should reflect a balance of positive and negative aspects of the organization's performance to enable a reasoned valuation of overall sustainability performance. The accuracy principle looks out for the correctness and low margin of error of the reported information. According to comparability principle, reports should enable stakeholders to analyse changes in the organization's performance over time and support comparative analysis to other organizations. Timeliness and clarity contains norms about the availability of the reported information. Timeliness individuates the need of the reporting process to follow a regular schedule of the information in order to be available in time for stakeholders to make informed decisions. The stakeholders may use the report if its information is under-

---

[20] GRI Standards, *GRI Universal Standards 100 series*, p. 7.

standable and accessible according to the clarity principle can use the information.

Finally, the information and processes used in the preparation of a report is gathered, recorded, compiled, analysed, and disclosed in a way that could be subject to examination and that ascertains its quality and materiality, the reliability principle is meet.

The second category of 100 series of the GRI Standard, that is called *"GRI 102: General Disclosures"*, is dedicated to the individuation of the information that is relevant to most organizations and interest most stakeholders. Standard disclosures are composed of six categories of reporting topics, setting up the overall context for reporting and decoding organizational performance in respect of six main area of disclosure: organization's strategy, profile, ethics and integrity, governance, stakeholder engagement and other reporting practice.

If the organization does not meet the minimum criteria stated in the standards for Core or Comprehensive, it cannot make a claim that its report has been prepared in accordance with the GRI Standards.

The third document, purpose of management approach disclosures is to cover how an organization addresses a given set of topics in order to provide context for understanding performance in a specific area. The 103 Standards includes general requirements and disclosures for reporting the management approach for material topics. It's the first set of principles of GRI that focuses on more detail description of the management approach to material topics, incorporating information on policies, commitments, goals and targets, responsibilities, resources, grievance mechanisms and specific actions that the organization uses. This information is set out and organized in the Standards as follows:

- General requirements for reporting the management approach;
- Disclosure 103-1 Explanation of the material topic and its boundary;
- Disclosure 103-2 The management approach and its components;
- Disclosure 103-3 Evaluation of the management approach.

The 200, 300 and 400 series deal with performance disclosures, both qualitative and quantitative that produce comparable information on the economic, environmental and social performance of the organization.

Accounting also means deriving indicators that enable organizations to define clear performance targets (Rasche and Esser, 2006) and their state of art through their on-going measurement.

Central to the social accounting framework is the use of performance indicators to measure the environmental, social and economic dimensions of sustainability. The use of indicators to estimate variables that cannot be measured precisely has a long history of use in environmental science

(Moldan et al., 1997), and is considered appropriate where variables that are inherently complex cannot be directly observed. The GRI Sustainability Accounting Standards proposes a wide array of data disclosures to measure performance toward the goal of sustainability. In particular, the 200, 300, 400 series of GRI Standards, encompass economic, environmental and social categories of disclosures providing specific indications for data representation in each topic-specific area. Each of the categories includes a set of core performance disclosures. GRI's multi-stakeholder processes are behind the development of the core disclosures: they are intended to identify generally applicable topics and are assumed to be material for most organizations. An organization following the GRI Standards should report on core indicators unless they are deemed not material on the basis of the reporting principles.

For each standard, three types of content are pinpointed:

1. Requirements that are mandatory for reporting on that specific topic. Some disclosures may have additional requirements on how to represent the information;

2. Actions that that are recommended but not required;

3. Guidance through which explanation and examples are provided. It may include background information, further explanation and examples.

The economic dimension of sustainability covers the organization's impacts on economic state of its stakeholders and on economic systems at local, national and international levels. The economic disclosures document – 200 series economic, includes six main categories of topics. According to these area, organizations should report data on: economic performance, market presence, indirect economic impacts, procurement practices, anti-corruption and anti-competitive behaviour.

The social performance disclosures – 300 series social, are divided into nineteen different categories: Employment, labour/management relations, occupational health and safety, training and education, diversity and equal opportunity, non-discrimination, freedom of association and collective bargaining, child labour, forced or compulsory labour, security practices, rights of indigenous peoples, human rights assessment, local communities, supplier social assessment, public policy, customer health and safety, marketing and labelling, customer privacy, socioeconomic compliance.

Within these topics, organizations are assisted to elaborate information. Some examples of specific social topics are: Occupational health and safety individuates indicators such as rates of injury, occupational diseases, lost days and absenteeism; Human rights assessment tries to evaluate the level to which human rights are considered in investment and supplier selection practices; The socioeconomic compliance concerns the compliance with laws and/or regulations and how the cases of non-compliance are managed.

A new topic introduced for the social disclosures by the new GRI set of standards, deals with management approach for supplier social assessment. According to this topic-related standard, the reporting organization shall report information on percentage of new suppliers that were screened using social criteria and on the negative social impacts in the supply chain and actions taken.

The last series 300 of topic – specific areas is composed by the environmental disclosures that cover performance related inputs and outputs. The eight categories of disclosures concern the performance related to biodiversity, environmental compliance and other relevant information such as environmental expenditure and the impacts of organization's products and services. In particular, they are grouped in the following topics: materials, energy, water, biodiversity, emissions, effluents and waste, environmental compliance and supplier environmental assessment. For all categories it is required specific data and information about the environmental behaviour and performance. Examples of information disclosures are materials used by weight or volume, percentage of materials used that are recycled, input materials, direct energy consumption, total water withdrawal and initiatives to mitigate environmental impacts of products and services.

An organization preparing a report in accordance with the GRI Standards can choose one of two options of compliance with the standards – Core or Comprehensive, depending on the degree to which the GRI Standards have been applied. For each option, GRI Standards provide a corresponding claim, or statement of use, that is required to the organization to include it in the report.

3.3.6. Integrated Reporting <IR>

Sustainability reporting can be subdivided into two broad categories. The first is a supplemental reporting to the traditional financial one that uses both quantitative and qualitative data that account to the expectations of broader categories of stakeholders (Coupland, 2006). The main difficulty encountered by the supplemental reports is to evaluate the relative materiality of social and environmental actions with respect to economic performance. Instead, the second category of sustainability reporting integrates social, environmental and economic data. In other words, the social and environmental dimensions are not supplemental to the financial accounts rather the three together are integral. Part of this approach can be considered the International Integrated Reporting. The GRI is one of the main supporter of the International Integrated Reporting Committee and considers integrated reporting to be the next step in sustainability reporting.

According to the International Integrated Reporting Council (IIRC) framework (Towards Integrated Reporting, 2011 and International <IR> Framework, 2013), Integrated Reporting brings together the material information about an organisation's strategy, governance, performance and prospects in a way that reflects the commercial, social and environmental context within which it operates (Cheng et al., 2014). It provides a clear and concise representation of how an organisation demonstrates stewardship and how it creates value, now and in the future. Integrated Reporting combines the most material elements of information currently reported in separate reporting strands (financial, management commentary, governance and remuneration, and sustainability) in a coherent whole, and importantly: shows the connectivity between them; and explains how they affect the ability of an organisation to create and sustain value in the short-, medium- and long-term. Summing up, the integrated report is not a "merged" report, where firms may represent a separate sustainability reporting section in its annual report without reflecting sustainability considerations in communicating its strategy, governance, risks and performance.

Integrated Reporting gives a broader explanation of organization's performance than traditional financial reporting. It makes visible an organization's use of and dependence on different resources and relationships or "capitals", its interaction with external factors, relationships and resources and the organization's access to and impact on them. For this analysis, IIRC individuates six capitals that the business may rely on, putting together the financial and non-financial resources [21]:

1. Financial capital: The wide-ranging of funds available to the organisation;

2. Manufactured capital: Manufactured physical objects, as distinct from natural physical objects;

3. Human capital: People's skills and experience, and their motivations to innovate;

4. Intellectual capital: Intangibles that provide competitive advantage;

5. Natural capital: Includes water, land, minerals, and forests; and biodiversity and eco-system health;

6. Social capital: The institutions and relationships established within and between each community, stakeholders and other networks to enhance individual and collective well-being. It includes an organisation's social license to operate.

---

[21] IIRC, *The International <IR> Framework*, 2013, Accessed 30 October 2018 at: http://integratedreporting.org/wp-content/uploads/2013/12/13-12-08-THE-INTERNATIONAL-IR-FRAMEWORK-2-1.pdf.

Reporting this information is critical to: a meaningful assessment of the long-term viability of the organization's business model and strategy; meeting the information needs of investors and other stakeholders; and ultimately, the effective allocation of scarce resources (De Villiers et al., 2014).

The IR and GRI work very closely together and their equivalent principles are closely aligned. Members of the IIRC and GRI Board and working groups overlap. Sustainability fundamentals are necessary to achieve integrated thinking and include:

– Understanding materiality;
– Incorporating multi-stakeholder considerations;
– Dealing with long-term issues and corresponding uncertainty;
– Selecting meaningful non-financial key performance indicators (KPIs).

GRI guidelines offer a detailed step-by-step process for firms that are new to sustainability. Thus, in companies that have gone through the GRI guidelines may have a much easier time meeting integrated reporting requirements. Note that this does not mean that a final report meeting GRI guidelines is required, but that the principles of GRI have been applied.

The main difference between the two standard is the target audience of IR. The primary audience of an Integrated Report are "providers of financial capital", which means investors and banks (IIRC, 2013). Specifically, it should be aimed at an investor who seeks long-term returns. GRI guidelines, on the other hand, do not specify a target audience and can be applied to a variety of stakeholders, including investors, employees, business partners, customers and non-profit organisations.

3.3.7. Auditing and assurance of the social performance – AA1000

Two of the main international standards for conducting external verification services on sustainability reports are the International Standard on Assurance Engagements (ISAE) 3000 issued by the International Auditing and Assurance Standard Board (IAASB), the issuing agency of the International Federation of Accountants (IFAC) and AccountAbility 1000 (AA1000 AS) issued in 2003 (with a second edition in 2008) by a British not for profit organization – The Institute of Social and Ethical Accountability (ISEA). Both these assurance standards are addressed to anyone who provides external verification services (Dando and Swift, 2003).

ISAE 3000 is the standard for assurance over non-financial information while AccountAbility 1000 is a voluntary standard for social and ethical accounting, auditing and reporting.

In particular, the AA1000 framework emphasized three principles[22]:

– completeness – that demand to the assurance provider to evaluate the extent to which the reporting organisation has included in its report material information on all of its activities, performance and impacts across all aspects of sustainability;
– materiality – requires that the assurance provider evaluate whether the reporting organisation has included adequate and timely information for the stakeholders;
– responsiveness – foster auditors to evaluate whether the reporting organisation has individuated and answered to stakeholder concerns, explained the basis of any strategy of reaction.

GRI framework also recommends the use of any internal resources that cover internal audit functions, internal controls and systems and in addition the external assurance for sustainability reports. Furthermore, the framework established some key qualities for external assurance, providing also the application levels that can be declared if external assurance was utilized for the report.

The review of the sustainability activities and reports, can individuate many benefits such as reinforce the credibility of sustainability reporting within stakeholders and investor groups, improving the quality of reported information and reporting processes.

3.3.8. ISO14000

ISO 14001 Environmental Management Systems (EMS) specifies the requirements an organization should meet in order to be certified by a third party. The standard has emerged as a leading management tool to address environmental issues at the firm level, that is confirmed by the rapid increase of its adoption worldwide as reported by international registrations to the Standard (MacDonald, 2005). The reasons for adopting this standard range from compliance oriented as in the case of the consumer pressure, to the economic oriented as in the case of potential cost savings.

The ISO 14001 Standard consists of the EMS specification and 17 clauses, reported under five categories of general requirements. Each clause was written to apply to a wide diversity of organizations, and is therefore not specific or prescriptive. The requirements describe general outcomes of the management system, but do not prescribe specific approaches an organization must implement to get there.

The domain of the principles, strategies, actions and tools is complex,

---

[22] AccountAbility, *AA1000AS Assurance Standard*, London, UK, 2008.

representing different issues and frameworks. They range from Cleaner Production and Pollution Prevention to Industrial Ecology and The Natural Step Framework, differing in scope, scale, intent and comprehensiveness.

With the ISO 14000 series, ISO standards deals with the area of organizational management that aim to create the basis for an international certification process for environmental management systems. ISO 14001 is not to measure any environmental effects of firms' activities or to ensure that those are minimized but it should be considered as a guide for identifying and managing performance criteria that are set by organizations implementing the standard[23]. It is a standard that identifies a process for managing company activities that have an impact on the environment. Organizations must have a procedure to review those activities in order to manage them efficiently. The main environmental aspects identified from the objectives set by the environmental management system, become the content of firm's policies and strategy, the target of operational controls, measurement and auditing.

Since the levels of the planning approach are critical to the EMS and the strategic planning can enhance further ISO 14001, they have been treated in different studies offering operative models for ISO 14000 (Robért, 2000; Robért et al., 2002).

3.3.9. Social Accountability 8000 (SA8000)

The SA8000 standard, introduced by the Council on Economic Priorities Accreditation Agency (CEPAA, 1997), is an auditable standard for a third-party verification system, to ensure both ethical sourcing of products and goods and workplace conditions worldwide.

SA8000 is applicable to any size of organization or business across all industry sectors. SA8000 is auditable for a third-party monitoring system through which the firm can receive certification if being compliant with the standard (Göbbels and Jonker, 2003). Facilities seeking to gain and maintain certification must go beyond simple compliance to integrate the standard into firms' management systems and practices through a Plan – Do – Check – Act model (Henkel, 2005) in a similar way as the ISO-standards (Larsen and Häversjö, 2001).

SA8000 is primarily based on the main conventions and recommendations of the International Labour Organization (ILO) and on the Universal

---

[23]Poksinska B., Jörn Dahlgaard J., Eklund J.A., *Implementing ISO 14000 in Sweden: motives, benefits and comparisons with ISO 9000*, International Journal of Quality and Reliability Management, 20(5), 585-606, 2003.

Declaration of Human Rights and the Convention on the Rights of the Child of the United Nations (UN). In particular, SA8000 standards encompasses the following topics:

1. child labour;
2. forced labour;
3. health and safety;
4. freedom of association and the right to collective bargaining;
5. discrimination;
6. disciplinary practices;
7. working hours;
8. compensation.

The SA8000 standard is accompanied by the Guidance Document (CEPAA, 1999) which helps with both the interpretation of the requirements and for the operative application of the requirements by the companies in the auditing process.

When applying SA8000 an organization must institute and adopt a Social Management System to ensure compliance and continuous improvement of the implementation of the abovementioned requirements. The SA8000 Social Management System, at the same way as the quality management system of the ISO standards, includes process stages of planning, implementation, checking and corrective actions and periodical management review.

The model illustrates both opportunities and challenges for the management as well as for the employees. By integrating these dimensions, Hart (2005) describes a four-field matrix that frames both the chances and challenges that management experiences when implementing SA8000. The internal activities of the model focus mainly on management perspectives of employee training and communication, risk reductions, costs and productivity improvements; while the external activities included in the model focus on corporate engagement with its external stakeholders in order to strengthen the reputation, legitimacy and growth. Stakeholders have an interest in the standard implementation process and consequently may affect the management through it (Roberts, 2003).

After analysing models' main characteristics, a classification is provided considering the information need expressed within the firm's prevailing patterns that they must fulfil in order to better match with the firms' specific configuration of social and economic dimensions.

Table 2. Social dimension measurement models' main characteristics.

The purpose of the measurement	The scale of the measurement process			
	Communication		Results	
	Internal	*External*	*Specific*	*Overall*
Regulation/Compliance	CM; GRI; SA8000	CM; GRI; IR; SA8000	CM; GRI; SA8000	CM; GRI; IR
Sustainability	GRI; BSC; CM; ISO14000	GRI; IR; CM; ISO14000	CM; GRI; ISO14000	CM; GRI; IR; BSC
Values/Mission	SA8000; BSC; SROI;	AA1000; SA8000; SROI;	AA1000; SA8000; SROI	AA1000; BSC
Welfare/Social Impact	SROI; VAS; BSC; SA8000	SROI; VAS; SA8000	SROI; SA8000	VAS; BSC

3.4. Social accounting process

Starting from the main characteristics that social accounting should represent, and considering the main features of the principal models for social accountability analysed in the previous sessions, a four steps process is proposed and analysed.

Referring to Gray's (2000) definition of social accounting, it involves: "… the preparation and publication of an account about an organisation's social, environmental, employee, community, customer and other stakeholder interactions and activities, and, where possible, the consequences of those interactions and activities. The social account may contain financial information but is more likely to be a combination of quantified non-financial information and descriptive, non-quantified information. The social account may serve a number of purposes but discharge of the organisation's accountability to its stakeholders must be clearly dominant of those reasons and the basis upon which the social account is judged …"[24]. The underlying goal of the social accounting process is to provide a level of stakeholder accountability, that is able, to account for and to be held accountable for the firm social and economic dimension, stakeholders' impacts and the ethical outcomes of management activities and for communicating these results to a broad set of stakeholders in firm's overall system.

Even though the process of social accounting is similar to the conventional financial accounting, it represents some distinctive key factors:

[24] Gray R.H., *Current developments and trends in social and environmental auditing, reporting and attestation: A review and comment*, International Journal of Auditing, 4(3), 247-268, 2000, p. 250.

– the focus is on the ethical, social and environmental data;
– the accountee are not only shareholders but a wide range of stakeholders;
– sustainability accounting is voluntary not yet regulated by law.

According to Adams (2004) "… rather than being concerned with profits and financial accountability, accountability as far as this article is concerned demonstrates corporate acceptance of its ethical, social and environmental responsibility. As such the "account" given should reflect corporate ethical, social and environmental performance …"[25].

Considering the main definitions and application of the concept of account and accountability in the field of corporate social and sustainability realm, the term social accounting will be used to refer to all accountability issues concerning the firms social dimension in a broad sense and therefore including also sustainability accounting that embraces the social, environmental and ethical accounting supporting and monitoring an organization's contribution towards or away from sustainability (Milne and Gray, 2013; Schaltegger et al., 2006). This is in line with Schaltegger and Burrit (2017) conceptualization that offer a broader definition of sustainability accounting describing it as a goal driven, stakeholder engagement process which attempts to build up a company specific measuring tool for sustainability issues and links between the social/environmental and economic dimensions.

The focus in this process is mainly on the rewards of the patterns that should be measured in order to properly manage the patterns in which they are embedded and to inform the parties that have provided the contributions to the firm.

---

[25] Adams C.A., *The ethical, social and environmental reporting – performance portrayal gap*, Accounting, Auditing and Accountability Journal, 17(5), 731-757, 2004, p. 732.

Figure 10. Rewards of social and economic patterns.

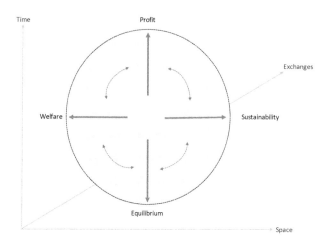

Even though the patterns are dynamic and should be considered as a whole, in order to facilitate the process of the accounting and especially the individuation of the object of measurement in the different patterns, a representation of the different categories of rewards is provided. Their interactions will depend on the configuration of firm's social and economic dimension in its overall system and may change in time and space as a result of the patterns' evolution.

In step 1 – *Data Gathering*, the process identifies the categories of data – values, environmental, social, and stakeholder information – to be gathered, and prioritized. Step 2 – *Data Evaluation*, proposes how to elaborate data in order to measure social and environmental benefits and costs and considers impacts on both firm social and economic dimension, both current state and future projections. Step 3 – *Reporting*, concerns the choice of the instruments through which "translate" and disseminate the information to stakeholders of the company, both internally and externally. Finally, step 4 – *Management Control*, focuses on the implementation of data in the decision-making process, in order to manage what was measured, ending the process of accounting and in the same time starting a new one.

Figure 11. Social Accounting Process.

3.4.1. Account identification and data gathering

As first step in the accounting process it is necessary for organizations to identify the right framework that better reflects the configuration of social and economic dimensions of the company as well as its industry and all the other factors encompassed in the firm's overall system. This phase of the process is influenced and depends on the main patterns individuated. In conventional accounting, most measures (although not necessarily all) are constructed around the data of economic performance such as those related to business performance (sales, profit, return on investment etc.), data on market presence, market penetration etc. In social accounting other more variegate and inclusive measures must be used to better understand, predict and take into account the increasing contributions, expectations, risks and opportunities companies' social dimension face referring to their exchanges in the overall system. These measures include: Environmental resources and impacts such as energy and water needed in productive processes, the percentage of waste, recycled of the materials, the amount of carbon emissions, etc.; Social resources can include labour indicators such as diversity, training or health and safety, etc. On a larger scale, other contributions might cover also data on topics such as product safety or community involvement.

A wide range of sustainability issues mapped out on industry level (as in the case of the standards of Sustainability Accounting Standard Board – SASB) or organized under the main categories of economic, environmental, social and governance (as in the case of Global Reporting Initiative – GRI reporting principles and standard disclosures), can be retrieved in the guidelines of the principal standards for social accounting.

In this first step, the organization must first identify all the broad groups of sustainability information required using the stakeholders' accountability perspective. The different issues related embedded in the patterns of firms' social dimension should then be prioritized considering their synergies with the economic dimension. This step depends also on how organizations decide their level of disclosure defined as the act of communicating organizational performance on material matters relating to financial, environmental, social and governance activities. Explaining how this prioritization has been achieved is an important part of the social accounting process (Lamberton, 2005).

The implementation of this phase of the process can be different for each organization because the configuration of the patterns of their social dimension, considering that the parties' contributions and expectations, that drive and define firms' activities, are different (for example due to geographical influences, industry specificities, ethical and cultural values, etc.). An adequate representation of these patterns in the firm's social dimension and their interaction with the economic one, is fundamental in this step. Furthermore, in order to better evaluate and prioritize the exchanges embedded especially in the patterns of social dimension, an inclusive approach concerning the main categories of parties involved – stakeholders and the community, is indispensable.

The selection and prioritization of the data, is influenced and influences on its turn organization's level of non-financial disclosure. Social and environmental disclosures as already seen, have been increasing in both size and complexity over the last decades. International studies, although indicating differences among countries (Michelon and Parbonetti, 2012; Gamerschlag et al., 2011; Orij, 2010), sectors (Toppinen et al., 2012, Pollach et al., 2009) and variation over time in the areas of disclosure (Reverte, 2009; Pava and Krausz, 1996), confirm the rise in the volume and importance of these disclosures (Gray et al., 2001). The identification of objective and transparent criteria that can help their prioritization is important for both the quality and efficiency of the hole process.

Considering the complexity and the importance of this step of the process, a three-questions test (Figure: 12) can be useful in order to target every single issue of the social dimension to the account that the organization aims to represent and communicate through the data analysis.

Figure 12. Individuation and "translation" of the data.

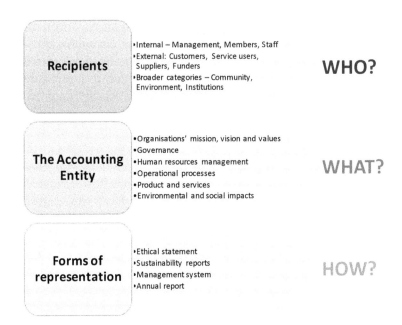

The individuation of the parties that are the potential recipient of the data, can answer to the first question: who will receive the information on the social performance of the organization? The distinction among internal, external and broader stakeholders or the community, is important not only for the selections of the data but also for its "translation". The information recorded should be made available in a manner that is understandable and accessible to all the parties that will use the information for evaluating if their expectation on the rewards are meet by the firm.

The second stage tries to answer to the question of what the organization do account for, defining the accounting entity for which the account data should be developed. The accounting entity can represent an area of organization's activities for which the information on the use of the existing and potential patterns' contributions to the firm, can be useful. In fact, the information provided by the data should help decision making of the entity to which it refers and should help the management and the corporate governance board of that entity, measure and report the efficient and effective use of the resources provided[26]. This test helps to select the social issues

---

[26] Adapted from the definition provided by the International Accounting Standards Board – *IASB Conceptual Framework 2010*, IFRS Foundation Publications Department, 2010.

considering the contribution in the impact-generation, that different organization's entities may have. In this way the process and the selection of the accounting data will be targeted to the patterns' main purposes.

Finally, the answer of the third question – how, provides the form of representation that the data must have, examining how the information can be translated in order to be communicated. This final stage should consider the better way to routinize the flows of data associated to exchange within patterns using appropriate tools and schemes. This test is important as not all the issues, especially those referring to the social dimension, can be put in numbers. Qualitative data, such as narratives that describe an organization's social and environmental impacts should be used as critical part of sustainability accounting (Lehman, 1999). The translation and modelling of the data will depend also on the typology of the rewards to which the reported information refers to (economic, sustainability, wellbeing, etc.). As a consequence, the social accounting information may also require forms of representation that includes qualitative explanations and storytelling in order to fit to the patterns within the information is exchanged. These "broader" forms of data representations include institutional reports, managerial control system information, web-based and social network communication, etc.

At the end of the first step, the data needed for measuring and evaluating the patterns' drivers and rewards, is selected.

3.4.2. Elaboration and evaluation of the data

The metrics of sustainability data should be part of a clear articulation of the casual relationships leading from the inputs to the process and then the flowing to the individuated outputs and outcomes (Epstein and Buhovac, 2014), and should be related to each pattern selected during the first step of the process. This step must individuate "… specific and appropriate measures that reflect the sustainability strategy are essential to monitor the key performance drivers (inputs and processes) and assess whether the implemented sustainability strategy is achieving its stated objectives (outputs) and thus contributing to the long-term success of the corporation (outcomes) …" [27].

During the second step of the social accounting process, organizations measure a broad set of social and environmental benefits and costs and consider their impacts on both their social and economic dimension. These evaluation activities include costs and benefits related to both current and future

---

[27] Epstein M.J., *Implementing corporate sustainability: Measuring and managing social and environmental impacts*, Strategic Finance, 89(7), 24-31, 2008, p. 165.

operations. The adoption of these models and measures, and the managerial systems needed to implement them, can help managers making more effective decisions to increase both sustainability and financial performance.

The process of evaluation often referrers to monetisation because in the conventional financial accounting the measurement is intended as the process of determining the monetary amounts at which the elements of the financial statements are recognised and carried in the balance sheet and income statement[28]. But financial units of measurement, that are the preferred choice for measuring economic performance, are not necessarily suitable for capturing social and ecological impacts, which require an array of measurement tools in order to capture nature's multiplicity of resource and impacts (Cooper, 1992) and the social impact generation or destruction. Measurability means expressing the indicator in terms that are measurable, rather than finding an indicator that is easy to measure[29]. Many social and environmental impacts may appear to have no market consequences and no financial effects, but many externalities are getting internalized in future perspective and do affect the operations and profitability of the firm in the long term even though the discount of their future effects are not measured. Furthermore, many economic benefits of sustainability are often seen as intangible assets and therefore difficult to measure. As a consequence, although some forms of social accounting rely on monetary units to measure environmental and social impacts, an increasing trend is the use of multiple units of measurement to assess performance toward the three dimensions of sustainability (Lamberton, 2005). The individuated patterns' in their dynamic evolution, represent complex and multidimensional issues that are not always directly measurable and require a set of indicators to enable performance evaluation toward their multiple objectives embedded in the patterns.

After evaluating the inputs and their effects and related expectations of the social and economic performance, organizations can develop and tailor appropriate models and mechanisms to measure their multiple results embedded in the firms' patterns. Several tools and techniques are already used to measure the different aspects of a social performance as already reported and analysed in this chapter. One of the theoretical model, that considers mostly the needs individuated at this step of the process, is the model offered by Epstein.

---

[28] IASB, *Conceptual Framework*, IFRS Foundation Publications Department, 2010, p. 37.

[29] The SROI Network, *A guide to social return on investment, Liverpool*, UK: SROI, 2012.

According to the Epstein's (2008, 2014) sustainability model, the managerial actions taken lead to sustainability performance and stakeholder reactions (outputs) that at a final stage affect long-term corporate financial performance (outcomes).

The long-term perspective is fundamental in this step. Bell and Morse (2012) point out that it is possible to distinguish between two categories of sustainability assessments: the first one more all-encompassing ("stronger") and the second ones that are more limited ("weaker"). The more all-encompassing ones, will set broader physical boundaries to the sustainability model, will refer to longer time frames for measuring stability and success, and will minimize trade-offs among the sustainability interest of competing components in the system. The broader the range of the activities involved and the longer the duration, the more the outcome will be affected by other factors and the measurement becomes complex.

Figure 13. Evaluation of resources and rewards.

In step 2, indicators should be developed and used to collect evidence on the selected drivers of the firms' performance in terms of inputs and processes, for evaluating the rewards produced in terms of outputs and outcomes, in both short and long term. These flows of inputs, processes, output and outcomes should be codified within the patterns of firms social and economic dimensions.

Usually the social value that is produced by firm's activities, is always measured as a positive result and rarely is reported as a value that is proportioned with the firms' objectives. The evaluation of the exchanges of the patterns must be done considering benefits in relation to their costs and the expectations of the parties involved, not in terms of benefits alone.

As represented in Figure 13, the first part of the evaluation deals with inputs that have immediate and identifiable costs and benefits that can affect long-term organization's performance. The second passage considers how the various inputs drive firm's performance through the management processes. The rewards produced are evaluated in terms of economic, social and environmental performances that directly impact the expectations of the parties involved in the process. Finally, a further evaluation should consider the entity of the social and economic results produced (output) compared to the objective set by the patterns' management and in accordance to its long-term mission (outcome).

Codifying and "translating" of the information is an important issue in this second step. The information is "translated" also in order to become intelligible for the stakeholder to whom is addressed (Zavani, 2000). Codifying enables the transmission of the information and identifies the tools that is more appropriated for data transfer.

3.4.3. Reporting and auditing

Following the designed process of social accounting that is driven by the target of stakeholder accountability, in the first two steps the core issues should be individuated and the performance measures related to the key contributions and the expected rewards, should be evaluated. This circular flow perspective of the social accounting process, individuates the requirement that accounting process cannot be separated from sustainability reporting and the strategic and operational management of social and environmental issues (Schaltegger and Burritt, 2017). In particular: "… reporting on sustainability and environmental social governance performance is a crucial step toward a market that rewards the creation of long-term wealth in a just and sustainable society …"[30].

Once the information is elaborated, the third component of the social accounting process concerns the dissemination of information to internal and external users. This process must be based upon three key questions:

– Which are the qualitative criteria that social accounting information should represent?

---

[30]Lydenberg S.D., Rogers J., Wood D., *From transparency to performance: Industry-based sustainability reporting on key issues*, Cambridge, MA, Hauser Center for Nonprofit Organizations, 2010, p. 10.

– What is the appropriate format of social accounting reports?

– Which are the communications tools and mechanisms that social accounting information should use for the internal and external disseminations?

Answering to these needs, influential standards and guidelines were developed to guide leading edge reporting practice. Many different institutions have released sustainability reporting frameworks. Some of them are issued by international organizations others by specific standard setters. A list of the principal models developed and their key characteristics were analysed in the previous paragraphs.

The growth of the adoption of voluntary sustainability reporting suggests that both corporations and their stakeholders find valuable information in the publication of this data. At the same time, the current trend in increasing levels of disclosure of organisations' social, ethical and environmental performance, is being undermined by a lack of confidence in both the data and the transparency of the reporting organizations (Doane, 2000). To bridge the critical credibility gap characterizing the reporting of sustainability, a strategic role is assigned to the assurance services provided by qualified auditors or audit companies (Milne and Adler, 1999, Dando and Swift, 2003, Manettiand and Becatti, 2009). The audit of the accounting process is a tool that is developed for both internal and external use for the verification of the reporting quality and that can foster stakeholder accountability is. The purpose of an audit has been defined as the investigation and review of actions, decisions, achievements, statements, or reports of specified persons with defined responsibilities, to compare these actions with norms, and to form and express an opinion on the result of that investigation, review and comparison (Power, 1996). Internally the audit can be seen as an important tool allowing the verification and enforcement of values and dynamics between the organization and its stakeholders. Based on this approach, the so-called social auditing is a dynamic process that an organisation follows to account for and improve its performance, consisting of planning, accounting, auditing and reporting, embedding and stakeholder engagement (Gao and Zhang, 2001). It provides a mechanism for decision-makers to evaluate environmental, ethical and social planning and facilitate stakeholder engagement in the social, environmental and ethical decision-making process of an organisation.

A match between corporate sustainability external auditing and internal social auditing, as both aim at improving the social, environmental and economic performance of organizations, can be an important tool for the accountability to a wider range of stakeholders and for the engagement of stakeholders in the accounting process.

The implementation of external assurance can be directed to professional providers, stakeholder panels and other external groups or individuals. The assurance process should follow given standards for assurance or they may involve approaches that follow systematic, documented and routinized processes. This process determines that the primary role of an audit is to provide the framework for an objective investigation of the quality of conduct of individuals and organizations compared with given sustainability standards, objectives or indicators.

3.4.4. Management control

Any strategy requires to be measured in terms of differences between the defined objectives and the results achieved from time to time, in order to understand if the company is moving in the right direction. In order to link and manage patterns of social and economic dimension simultaneously, the need to measure and confront complex results arises. Many companies have introduced measurement systems to evaluate their social and environmental performance without considering their potential benefits in terms of managerial control of financial results in relation to social strategies related objectives. The setting up of these objectives should bring out the interaction between social values, corporate values and economic values going beyond the measurement systems that focus only on social and environmental sustainability and analysing the impact of firm's activities, on the reputation or compliance with the rules. What companies currently measure to demonstrate the impacts of their activities can be a valuable means of informing, but it does not however coincide with what they should measure to detect the value creation. For example, standards-based sustainability indicators certainly help companies to raise awareness about the impact of their operations on society, but the emphasis is still on the full range of possible impacts and demonstration of progress made.

Accounting data is used by organizations in internal and external governance processes. In particular, internal uses of accounting information arise from the need to measure and control activities and to assist with data the decision-making processes. As suggested by the Corporate Sustainability Model, developed by Epstein and Buhovac (2014) reported previously, the alignment of strategy, structure, management systems and performance measures is fundamental for organizations to coordinate activities and motivate employees toward implementing a sustainability strategy.

"… The management of sustainability performance requires a sound management framework which, on the one hand, links environmental and social management with the business and competitive strategy and management and, on the other hand, integrates environmental and social information with economic business information and sustainability reporting ..."[31]. Referring to this function of the social accounting process, the measurement of the value embedded in the patterns of social dimension, should not replace the current measurement approaches in management accounting but rather integrate their perspective, in order to manage them dynamically with the patterns of the economic dimension.

Social and environmental concerns, related to stakeholders' expectations, must be related to traditional financial and economic goals, developing a multidimensional and inclusive performance measurement system. This can help firm's performance to be evaluated in a holistic, and balanced approach, assisting managers to guide decision-making and corporate behaviour. Since the formulation and implementation of social strategy can lead to the improvement of competitive advantage and enhance economic performance, companies should make use of appropriate management systems to manage, measure and monitor the strategic objectives and results achieved in both social and economic dimension. Similarly, a sustainability performance management and measurement system is defined as: "... the measurement and management of the interaction between business, society and the environment ..."[32]. The social dimension perspective may add to this system the interaction among patterns through the circularity of the triadic exchanges of stakeholder – contribution – expectations that they represent in each dimension.

Once the data is reported, during the management control process can be evaluated the sustainability performance comparing the results achieved with the objectives individuated during the planning phase. This is an important assessment practice as it can individuate important improvements to add to the firms' activities and revisit the targets in setting out the new objectives.

In this last step, the role of social accounting measurement (Schaltegger and Burritt, 2010) is to:

1. Support the process of engaging management in the development and improvement of firm social dimension;

2. Review the results, processes and inputs as well as to relate these areas to each other;

3. Support and challenge management in their choosing measures of social dimension;

4. Facilitate communication and review of social accounting reports.

---

[31] Schaltegger S., Wagner M., *Integrative management of sustainability performance, measurement and reporting*, International Journal of Accounting, Auditing and Performance Evaluation, 3(1), 1-19, 2006, p. 2.

[32] *Ibidem*, p. 3.

The information provided, in the management control step, can be elaborated also for a single processes or products and services giving a single measure for the sustainability of the unit analysed.

The adequate information system and tools can be implemented considering the accounting process and the sustainability standards that focus on both the content and the process of the creation of the accounting documents.

Even though many normative and standards require the individuation of the adequate management control framework for social and environmental issues, their integration within the firms' strategy and accounting process, remains still a big challenge for firms' management. Grounding this process in the patterns' configuration, can help the integration of these issues with the economic ones and bring them closer to firm's strategy.

Chapter 4

INNOVATIVE STARTUPS WITH A SOCIAL GOAL (ISSG)

4.1. The social and economic dimensions in the case of Innovative Startups with a Social Goal

As a result of the alternative approaches to sustainable economic development, the concept of the traditional corporate form has evolved, bringing about a new understanding of how people think of and evaluate businesses. The rise of new forms of organization requires a redefinition and reconfiguration of the fundamental patterns that constitute business activities.

Hybrid organizations, and especially social entrepreneurship, have become a topic of great importance during the last few years, especially in the light of the many successful examples from all over the world and a variety of sectors, fuelling the debate amongst the business community, academics and legislators (Boschee 2006; Nicholls 2006). More specifically, Social Enterprises, by virtue of their hybrid nature, are required to achieve both social and financial performance (Ebrahim, et al., 2014). These two dimensions also coexist in traditional firms and non-profit organizations, which, as we saw previously, have also increasingly begun to measure their performance in these spheres. However, social enterprises that combine social and profitmaking activities in their mission can pose a crucial challenge in identifying a management approach based on and fitted to their prevailing patterns, since their definition of success includes both dimensions and the synergies they can support.

The importance of research into the topics of Social Entrepreneurship and Social Enterprises is reflected by the growing number of articles and books on these subjects (Dacin et al. 2010; Short et al. 2009s; Haugh, 2006; Light, 2006; Mair and Marti, 2006; Mair et al., 2006; Perrini, 2006; Ebrahim et al., 2014; Wry et al., 2017). At the same time, the study of social entrepreneurship has developed along different lines [1] in the US (Henton et al., 1997; Brinckerhoff, 2000; Dees et al., 2001; Drayton, 2002), in the UK (Leadbeater, 1997; Social Enterprise UK, 2013) and in continental Europe (Defourny and Nyssens, 2008; Defourny and Nyssens, 2010; Kerlin, 2006; Borzaga and Defourny, 2004). In the US and UK, attention has focused on the "commercialization" of the non-profit sector and the creation of private firms supplying goods and services for public welfare. In continental Europe, however, attention has been concentrated much more on community entrepreneurship, and the phenomenon has been studied mainly at an organizational level (Defourny and Nyssens 2008).

These social ventures embody characteristics of both the for-profit and the not-for-profit sectors. The tendency in social enterprise management is to add an economic perspective to socially oriented activities undertaken in response to a social need, in order to scale the solution they can offer. The connections between dimensions found in the different forms of Social Enterprise can allow analysis of the various possible configurations of different integration and synergies across dimensions.

Therefore, the decision to analyze the configuration of the social and economic dimensions in these forms of organizations arises from the need to examine both the antecedents and the consequences of integrated management of the two dimensions, and the alignment between them of both social and financial performance.

By applying the framework proposed in this study, we can test the ability of Innovative Startups with a Social Goal and Benefit Corporations to capture, evaluate and study the management of the value produced in the specific configuration of their patterns (linked to both the social and the economic dimensions) and also make comparisons between them. This approach enables us not only to consider two different models of hybridization of the social and economic dimensions, but also to capture their characteristics in two different stages of the firm's development – startups and established firms.

In addition to the configuration of the two dimensions, the analysis of the relative social impact measurement and assessment models and tools can foster and identify new issues for the future development of the social accounting process. As already described in the previous chapters, while methods for assessing financial performance are well established, the as-

---

[1] For complete reviews on SE, definitions can be found in Short J.C., Moss T.W., Lumpkin G.T., *Research in social entrepreneurship: Past contributions and future opportunities*, Strategic entrepreneurship journal, 3(2), 161-194, 2009; Zahra S.A., Gedajlovic E., Neubaum D.O., Shulman J.M., *A typology of social entrepreneurs: Motives, search processes and ethical challenges*, Journal of business venturing, 24(5), 519-532, 2009.

sessment of social performance is variegated and lacks standardization and comparability (Ebrahim and Rangan, 2014; Paton, 2003).

4.2. Social and economic dimensions in Social Enterprises

The terms "Social Enterprises" and "Social Entrepreneurship" – SE – first appeared in the literature in the 1960s (Thompson, 2008). However, only in the last twenty years have these concepts started to spread, thanks especially to the Ashoka Foundation (founded in 1981) and other pioneer organizations in the field of social entrepreneurship. The term Social Entrepreneurship has been defined through a multiplicity of concepts and perspectives. For example, Gawell et al. (2009) refer to Social Entrepreneurship as a set of initiatives which aim to improve what is missing or non-functioning in society, including new solutions that aim to create a sustainable economic, social and ecological society by adopting an entrepreneurial logic. Another definition, proposed by Sullivan Mort et al. (2003), views Social Entrepreneurship as a multidimensional construct encompassing entrepreneurially virtuous behaviours to achieve social goals. According to this conceptualization, it could be affirmed that, in general, social enterprises use innovative ways of solving important social problems, by combining the creation of social and shared value with economic value-generation – they cover the void between business and social themes, with the objective of serving the community and society, rather than obtaining maximum profit.

Dart (2004) asserts that social enterprise differs from the traditional interpretation of non-profit organizations from a strategic, structural and moral point of view[2] – it represents a radical innovation of the social dimension of firms.

Hartigan's definition (2006) highlights the fact that a social enterprise's principal objectives are not related to profit maximization and the growth of shareholders' financial return, but require them to serve and efficiently satisfy the needs of the largest possible number of disadvantaged people. In this sense, he notes that financial capital accumulation is not a priority for social enterprise[3].

For Korosec and Berman (2006), an SE is an organization, group or community, in which people come together to develop new processes and

---

[2] Dart R., *The legitimacy of social enterprise*, Nonprofit management and leadership, 14(4), 411-424, 2004.

[3] Hartigan P., *It's about people, not profits*, Business Strategy Review, 17(4), 42-45, 2006.

new services, with the purpose of finding the best solutions for specific social problems, answering the needs of particular classes of poor individuals[4].

In their evolutional theory of economic change, in which the leverage for change is applied by mechanisms of natural economic selection, produced by the market, which defines the success of enterprises in terms of growth and capacity for survival, Nelson and Winters (2009) offer some important considerations for SE[5]. They describe the social enterprise as an evolution of the traditional enterprise form that goes beyond the objective of generating profits, with the aim of offering services for culture, social benefits, health and education.

Finally, a definition that puts together and combines many of the different aspects pointed out by the different definitions delineates SE as organizations whose purpose is to achieve a social mission through the use of market mechanisms (Mair and Marti, 2006; Kerlin, 2010; Santos, 2012). Therefore, an important feature that can help in the identification and construction of SEs is: "… Their primary objective is to deliver social value to the beneficiaries of their social mission, and their primary revenue source is commercial, relying on markets instead of donations or grants to sustain themselves and to scale their operations …"[6]. These elements are represented by the main components of the theoretical framework based on the firm's social and economic dimension patterns, confirming the potential utility that its configuration may offer for management structures and tools in different types of organizations.

4.2.1. The development of Social Enterprises: different contexts, different paths

Although social entrepreneurship and social enterprises have met with widespread approval over the years, their definition is still highly context-dependent, meaning that different interpretations are possible; the main difficulty is that social entrepreneurship is a contingent combination of activities, which various researchers have set out to interpret and measure (Bacq and Janssen 2011; Nicholls 2010).

Bacq and Janssen (2011) try to represent different approaches applied to the SE field, adopted in different cultures in different areas of the world, as a consequence of the spread of the social entrepreneurship phenome-

---

[4] Korosec R.L., Berman E.M., *Municipal support for social entrepreneurship*, Public Administration Review, 66(3), 448-462, 2006.

[5] Nelson, R.R., Winter S.G., *An evolutionary theory of economic change*, Harvard University Press, 2009.

[6] Ebrahim A., Battilana J., Mair J., *The governance of social enterprises: Mission drift and accountability challenges in hybrid organizations*, Research in Organizational Behavior, 34, 81-100, 2014, p. 82.

non. The different types of SE are identified by means of the intersection of three spheres, representing[7]:

- the market – referring especially to small businesses and the private sector;
- the State – representing the importance of local/national government;
- civil society – referring to all registered charities, development and non-governmental organizations, community groups, women's organizations, faith-based organizations, professional associations, trade unions, self-help groups, social movements, business associations, coalitions and advocacy groups.

The prevalent European model of SE is located in the space between "Market" and "State", because the phenomenon of social entrepreneurship was born and has developed thanks to the support of national governments and the guidance of European Union Policy. This clearly emerges in the study by Borzaga and Defourny (2004), which offers a general review of the European situation, initially highlighting the characteristics that link social enterprises' operations to two main principles: employment integration and the distribution of social services for communities and people. In this definition, academics identified a relationship between the development of the first forms of social entrepreneurship in the '70s and the contextual and contemporary decrease in the economic growth rate and rise in unemployment. The study considers the differentiation of social enterprise models among countries from Western European and Eastern European. In the first group, the development and spread of social enterprises was a consequence of the crisis of the Welfare State and the awareness of the difficulties in financing public services, and also a result of its increasing inability to satisfy civil society's needs.

The growth of SE happened very spontaneously, without any real transfer of property from public to private hands: the State continues to support projects, but is no longer capable of acting unaided or of being the sole provider of the services required. In fact, there are many, consolidated procedures by which the state finances the provision of social services, through subsidies, negotiated fixed prices or user refunds.

When defining the SE phenomenon and its main distinctive characteristics with reference to specific contexts, mention must be made of the work of Muhammad Yunus, Nobel Peace Laureate in 2006 and 2010. He is a Bengali economist and banker, already famous for being the inventor of modern microcredit, which allows people living in extreme poverty and marginalization to access financial services for entrepreneurial purposes.

---

[7] Nyssens M., *Social Enterprise - At the Crossroads of Market, Public Policies and Civil Society*, Routledge, New York, 2006.

He is also well-known for being the author of "Building Social Business. The new kind of capitalism that serves humanity's most pressing needs"[8], which clearly outlines the position of modern social enterprises, somewhere between traditional profit-oriented enterprises and non-profit charitable organizations, and offers a clear explanation of how the social firm takes its means from the former and its ends from the latter. According to Yunus, in general there are two types of enterprises that have social purposes: the first are firms oriented to the resolution of social problems, which do not distribute dividends but invest their profits in the implementation and improvement of the social activities they carry out; while the second are, in general, firms that are profit-oriented, but whose ownership is controlled, directly or indirectly, exclusively by people who live in a high level of poverty, need and social disadvantage. The Grameen Bank puts Yunus's theories into practice: in 1976 he founded the first bank specifically intended to supply microcredit in Bangladesh and India, offering small credits, without demanding guarantees, to poor, local populations. The system is based on trust and the idea that these people have entrepreneurial capabilities that can potentially be effective in creating both economic and social value, if they are financed.

When we look for other concepts similar to that proposed by Muhammad Yunus, it is interesting to turn to the work of Italian academics Borzaga and Fazzi (2008), who summarize the definitions of social enterprise available in the literature in three main context-related groups[9], one of them corresponding exactly to the idea put forward by Yunus. Starting from this category, it is possible to identify a type of social enterprise born in a context of underdeveloped economies, grinding poverty and social diseases, communities in which the Welfare State is not efficient or collaborative.

The first and second groups are different from the third, which we have just examined, and there are many differences between them, due to the diversity of the contexts in which they have developed. The first definition has Anglo-Saxon origins and originated in a context principally in favour of traditional profit-oriented, short-lived firms, but also with a Welfare State which plays only a limited role. American culture, in particular, is strongly based on the certainty that the abilities and capabilities of the individual are the main source of entrepreneurial success. This type of social enterprise is located in this context, trying to cover the void caused by a lack of public sector resources and insufficient donations, to enable people to increase

---

[8] Yunus M., *Building social business: The new kind of capitalism that serves humanity's most pressing needs*, Public Affairs, 2011.

[9] Borzaga C., Fazzi L., *Governo e organizzazione per l'impresa sociale*, Carocci, Roma, 2008.

their own development by managing productive activities that can generate profits for subsequent investment in social activities. In America, especially, there is a strong concept of the social entrepreneur, linked to leadership and a flair for business innovation. In this sense, it could be affirmed that this first type of definition accepts a wider, extensive, flexible concept of the social enterprise.

The second definition originated in the European context. It differs from the previous one, due to a more active Welfare State, private organizations that offer services for social purposes and non-traditional forms of enterprise. In this context, the social enterprise is located within in a specific institutional environment, having a greater social commitment, longer working relationships and collective forms of control and operation.

Another important feature found in the literature is that SEs may take a variety of legal forms, some of them hybrids of the traditional ones, generally depending on the legal framework in the different countries concerned (Ebrahim et al, 2015). The Italian literature offers other important studies (Borzaga and Defourny, 2004; Andorlini and Ciappei, 2011), affirming that a social enterprise is a combination of complex parties in continuous evolution, with the objective of promoting social benefit, reinforcing welfare systems, and sustaining people affected by social diseases and rejected by society, while implementing their activity through the use of the typical tools of business economics[10]. In general, the field consists of small organizations with highly democratic connotations, often using voluntary work or forms of assistance, enjoying strong relationships with local government and sometimes using private donations, due to the fact that they are almost exclusively engaged on the production of goods and services for a social purpose. Their social objectives can thus also be described as strategic, because they do not only organize single charity events, but aim to become part of the economic fabric, to support transactions between private and public parties and develop a significant, lasting distributive function. The social needs of the relevant target stakeholders engage and overlap with the complex economic processes traditionally intrinsic to any business. The link with local communities is fundamental: the connection between entrepreneurs, territory and community is essential to meet social needs not only from a quantitative perspective, but also through the continuous improvement in the quality of the outputs offered. This link must be developed to fulfil the challenging mission of the social dimension: to promote, encourage and improve the welfare of the stakeholders who are the providers of its resources and recipients of its rewards.

Another contribution to the debate on different SE configurations was

---

[10] Andorlini C., Ciappei C., *Imprenditorialità sociale tra sviluppo di comunità e creazione di valore*, Picini Editore, 2011.

provided by Massetti (2008), who classifies the different types of SE in a matrix based on the idea proposed by Drayton (2002), which considers the social enterprise as a new form of organization, which cannot be assimilated to other existing entrepreneurial forms. It could be defined as a complex system with main aspects and objectives that are usually changeable [11] and not always classifiable in a single combination.

According to his classification, different types of social enterprise can be placed in the four quadrants of a matrix with the mission of the socially oriented entrepreneurial project on the vertical axis and its economic purposes on the horizontal one. On the basis of the combination of these two drivers, the first category consists of non-profit firms and those with a socially oriented mission, such as traditional social organizations, non-profit organizations, foundations and social cooperatives, while a contrasting second category comprises traditional profit-oriented and market-oriented organizations. The third grouping represents organizations that are market-oriented, but do not work to create profit, and thus have to access support through alternative financing instruments. Finally, the fourth and last category contains organizations that meet social needs by pursuing profits and the improvement of both social and economic sustainability.

In this realm, the relative configurations of the social and economic dimensions, as defined through the identification and combinations of their main patterns, can help to increase understanding of SEs' emerging "unconventional" business processes and aid the formulation of appropriate models for their value creation and performance management. The dynamic nature of the patterns of the two dimensions and their interrelationships can be more effective in detecting and representing SEs' drivers and defining the archetype in which their operations place them. Although there are a variety of approaches and definitions of SE, the foundations of the process by which the social dimension is configured in SEs can be traced in the common features which define the boundaries of social entrepreneurship (Martin and Osberg, 2007). All definitions of social entrepreneurship agree that social and environmental issues and results must be given top priority, with the maximization of profit and other strategic considerations taking a secondary role. This "social utility" is expressed not only through the creation of public goods and positive externalities, but also through new organizational processes. Another common characteristic is innovation and especially social innovation: it may be pursued through new organizational models and processes, and new products and services, or a new way of

---

[11] Massetti B.L., *The social entrepreneurship matrix as a "tipping point" for economic change*, Emergence: Complexity and Organization, 10(3), 1, 2008.

conceiving and defining society's demands. Finally, many authors point out that social entrepreneurs promote their socially innovative models through market-oriented actions, where economic performance is of primary importance, while extending their projects into other contexts, through alliances and partnerships, with the idea of achieving broader, more sustainable results (Weerawardena and Mort, 2006). These three aspects make up what Nicholls and Cho (2006) identify as the main constituent elements of social enterprise: sociality, innovation and market orientation. All these elements were analysed in the conceptualization of the firm's social dimension, but due to the particular role that sociality, in terms of social context and communities, has in the definition and activities of SE, additional analysis of its influence in SE will be provided.

4.2.2. Community – culture – rewards patterns in Social Entrepreneurship

The concept of "Community" has already been specified in previous chapters as one of the main determinants of the patterns of the firm's social dimension, especially in relation to the cultural values that influence its management models and processes and shape the creation and development of many patterns. In this section, the concept of "Community" and the patterns in which it is expressed are analyzed in the light of its specific contribution to social entrepreneurship.

A community consists of individuals linked together by a variety of motivations. In a literature review of definitions of community, Hillery (1955) found that most of the definitions analysed cited social interaction, geographic area and common ties as essential elements of community life. Another important issue for defining communities, often cited by the studies reviewed, was social interaction. Subsequently, other definitions, offered mainly by the social science literature, confirm the importance of these factors, while putting greater emphasis on the last key point, which highlights the importance of the existence of common ties within a common geographic area[12]. Applying the concept of community in the identification and resolution of social problems such as health issues, Patrick and Wickizer (1995) offered an operative definition of community, viewed as "… the entire complex of social relationships in a given locale, and their dynamic interaction and evolution in working toward [the] solution of health problems …"[13].

---

[12] Willis C.L., *Definitions of community, II: an examination of definitions of community since 1950*, South Sociologist, 9, 14-19, 1977.

[13] Patrick D.L., Wickizer T.M., *Community and health*, in Amick B.C., Levine S.,

In general, a community is characterized mainly by the relational interactions or social ties that draw people together [14]. Very often, the success of a community also depends on the sharing of physical location, which keeps its members close together: in this sense a local community is a group that is mainly recognizable and potentially more able to solve social problems. Generally, individuals also share the same cultural values, meaning that they are in the same conditions to recognize the same behaviours, understand the same languages, and as a result build up uniform patterns within the organizational social and economic dimensions, reflected in the way in which they respond to their common social needs. The main difficulty for organizations is how to manage these relationships, expressing them through a group of people who share the same values, with the aim of dealing with new challenges, raising awareness of needs and guaranteeing sustainable answers to community welfare issues, through sustainable entrepreneurial activities.

The earlier analysis of the main definitions of SE indicated that the objectives of social entrepreneurship projects include the pursuit of collective benefits while meeting the social needs that are typically expressed within a community. Furthermore, "… the pursuit of collective benefits associated with the goods or services produced constitutes one of the incentives and explains the commitment of the individuals who create the social enterprise …" [15]. What's more, since they live together in the same geographic area, individuals of a given community share common traits in their identity, expectations and interests (Marquis and Battilana, 2009), which in some cases can facilitate and even be vital for SE activities (Seelos et al., 2011) [16]. Therefore, essential aspects of the management of communities in SE projects are social competences and the ability to link them to business management in order to run and sustain the project. This is one of the categories of patterns considered in the firm's social dimension, in which the concept of community perfectly matches the processes of community-related outcome generation found in SE.

Tarlov A.R., Walsh D.C., *Society and Health*, New York, NY, Oxford University Press Inc, 46-92, 1995, p. 51.

[14] Heller K., *Return to community*, American Journal of Community Psychology, 17(1), 1-15. 1989.

[15] Jean-Louis l., Marthe Nyssens M., *The social enterprise Towards a theoretical socioeconomic approach*, in Borzaga C., Defourny J., *The emergence of social enterprise*, Vol. 4, Psychology Press, 2004, p. 315.

[16] Seelos C., Mair J., Battilana J., Dacin T.M., *The embeddedness of social entrepreneurship: Understanding variation across local communities*, in *Communities and organizations*, Emerald Group Publishing Limited, 2011.

In this perspective, it is important to note that technological evolution and the introduction of the Internet have led to a new concept of community, the "Virtual Community," where the sharing of physical spaces among members is not a necessary condition for community building. It is also important to consider patterns developed online, as "... Online social networks have become a parallel community for many, satisfying in the virtual world the impulse to sociability in man. ... it brings an opportunity for other business to develop from the additional information about the network participants and their interests ..." [17]. Efficient virtual communication, allowing the exchange of information concerning common interests and objectives, has also permitted the development of this further conceptualization of communities, based on common elements that are not necessarily linked to the area where people live. This perspective adds many more features to the concept of community, such as the sharing of a common identity, based on the common presence of particular and specific interests and aspects, and ideals, shared traditions and the achievement of precise objectives. The development of virtual communities is dependent on the creation of bases for the users to participate actively, with the maximum effort and the maximum drive to improvement, implying the opportunity to use the SEs' products and/or services, or other types of outputs, which facilitate the encounter between individuals and the exchange of information, opinions and mutual help.

The central point that relates social enterprises to communities may lie in the strategy that enterprises adopt to create a sense of identification and responsibility amongst their stakeholders, who are also the recipients of their activities. These groups of people and resources are oriented towards the identification of unsatisfied social needs, with the aim of creating the organizational structures needed to provide efficient, sustainable answers to them. It is thus possible to create a system capable of operating productively and sustainably, not completely dependent on external parties, and potentially able to influence the decision-making mechanisms of complex stakeholder – contributions – rewards patterns. The identification and configurations of social dimension patterns becomes a crucial resource in terms of the detection of social needs and the expansion of opportunities. It is thus important to define the enterprise's mission in collaboration with stakeholders and communities, activating the engagement process through the exchanges within the patterns as previously described. The adoption of

---

[17] Ganley D., Lampe C., *The ties that bind: Social network principles in online communities*, Decision Support Systems, 47(3), 266-274, 2009, p. 266; Citation in the reported text is from: Simmel G., Frisby D., M. *Featherstone, Simmel on Culture: Selected Writings*, Sage Publications Inc., 1997.

the social dimension analysis framework may enable engagement to be given formal structures, by means of more stable procedures and multi-stakeholder governance systems.

When these characteristics of SE are transposed into the social dimension framework, the configuration of patterns generated within the two dimensions and including the various resources and rewards will prevail. Adopting the multi-dimensional approach identified earlier and focusing on three key defining features of social entrepreneurship and the potentially crucial role of the communities in which SEs develop, the next section will analyse social and economic configurations and their measurement in the case of a specific form of SE in a given context: Italian Innovative Startups with a Social Goal (ISSG) and Benefit Corporations.

4.3. The Italian SE context – Innovative Startups with a Social Goal (ISSG)

This section examines SE in the Italian context in order to define common ground for cultural, community, institutional and market drivers, since over several decades the country has witnessed first the introduction and then the expansion of innovative models of social enterprise, in a variety of legal forms, as an integral part of its economic life. The scenario has been further reinforced by the creation of new legal forms of organization which are absolute firsts on the international economic stage. The following is a brief overview of the main forms of social enterprise introduced during the last few years, highlighting the opportunities and needs which each of them implies.

Legislative Decree no. 155/2006 introduced the definition of a social enterprise into Italian law, as any privately owned firm whose business is the exchange of socially useful goods and services.

In particular, a social enterprise must satisfy the following conditions:

– its business must be in the areas of education and training (scholastic and non-scholastic), protection of the environment and ecosystem, promotion of the cultural heritage, social tourism, university and postgraduate education, research and cultural services, services to social enterprises, and social, health and community health services;

– there must be no distribution of profits to shareholders, since the enrichment pursued by a social enterprise is the improvement in quality of life of the community within which it operates.

Of the various types of organisations that make up the third sector, social enterprises are the most market-oriented, since they operate as normal businesses and employ workers, at least 50% of whom, the law states, must be paid (i.e. not unpaid volunteers).

Generally, Italian social enterprises are incorporated as social cooperatives (under Law 381/1991). Cooperatives differ from other companies in their mutualistic goals, since their mission is to provide their members (rather than shareholders) with goods, services or employment opportunities. Social cooperatives have the added purpose of pursuing the general good of the community as a whole, the promotion of humanitarian values and social integrations, and they can therefore only operate through specific forms:

• type A social cooperative: for the provision of health and social services and educational services;
• type B social cooperatives: engaging in other businesses – agricultural, industrial, retail or services – and established to create jobs for the disadvantaged, who must make up at least 30% of the labour force;
• "mixed" social cooperatives: meeting the requirements of both types A and B – a much smaller category.

One very interesting category of social enterprise examined in this study is that of innovative startups with a social goal (ISSG). Italian Decree Law 179/2012 introduced a new body of legislation governing the foundation and growth of innovative startups. Specifically, article 25, subsection 2 defines an innovative startup as a capital enterprise, which may also be a cooperative, incorporated under Italian law, shares or stakes in which are not listed on a regulated market or on a multilateral trading system, which meets specific requirements. Within this broader definition of an innovative startup, the Law identifies two additional types of enterprise which are awarded greater fiscal benefits for their potential investors: startups with social goals and high-tech startups in the energy industry.

To allow the testing and verification of the social dimension model's main configurations and features, the focus is on a single form of organization – ISSGs operating in specific domains of particular social value according to Italian legislation. Furthermore, the importance of innovation in the definition of these enterprises enables us to test the appropriateness and efficiency of the social dimension framework in managing and measuring innovation-oriented activities.

Thus, the analysis will be focused on a type of enterprise which has distinctly social and innovation characteristics from its foundation, and is therefore in need of a management process capable of identifying, measuring and managing social dimension patterns. This measurement process becomes an integral part of the company's make-up, without which it would lose its social vocation and thus its legal status and the tax concessions granted by the law.

4.4. The configuration of an ISSG's social and economic dimensions

From the operational point of view, a social startup must meet all the criteria for innovative startups and also fulfil an additional condition related to its area of business, in order to qualify as such. In particular, for ISSGs it is mandatory to comply with the "cumulative" prerequisites (meaning that they must all be fulfilled) listed in the aforesaid article 25, subsection 2, and the "alternative" prerequisites in the same point.

The cumulative prerequisites are summarised below:

• the company must have been incorporated, and have been engaging in the business concerned, for no more than 60 months, meaning 5 years;
• it must have its registered office and operations centre in Italy;
• from the innovative startup's second year in business, the total value of annual production must not exceed 5 million Euro;
• it must not distribute or have distributed profits;
• its exclusive or prevalent corporate purpose must be the development, production and sale of innovative, high-tech products or service;
• it must not have been incorporated from a merger or corporate break-up, or further to the transfer of ownership of a company or company division;
• it must operate in the sectors envisaged by the law, as described above.

These criteria set up a clear map of the parties and their involvement in ISSGs' activities. In particular, the role of the shareholders of the ISSG is not only of equity-provider but they should also be committed to the social cause the firms pursue and support the development of social innovation. In terms of rewards they do not prioritise profit generation as the company cannot distribute profits for its first 5 years in business. The ISSG's shareholder rewards are influenced by the social impact produced, since this can also determine the entity and sustainability of medium-long term economic performance. As a result, in the case of ISSGs, the shareholders – equity – profit patterns are similar to those of the economic dimension (stakeholder – resources – sustainability) and in some cases, depending on the social purposes and the mission of the ISSG, they may be exactly the same.

Moving on to the second category of requirements (which are alternatives), the law requires the company to fulfil at least one of the following conditions:

• it must spend at least 15% of the cost or total value of its production (whichever is greater) on research and development;

• at least one third of the total workforce must consist of highly qualified people, who may be formal employees or freelance associates of any
kind;

• it must be the owner, registered holder or licensee of at least one pa-
tent.

In order to encourage the creation and development of startups with
social goals and high-tech energy industry startups, Italian legislation grants
potential investors a higher rate of tax concessions. For both types of
startups, the law grants:

– tax deduction of 25% for investors who are natural persons up to a
maximum investment of Euro 500,000 on an annual basis;

– tax deduction of up to 27% for investors who are legal persons up to
a maximum annual investment of Euro 1,800,000.

Under these conditions, economic resources are strictly related to social
ones: the investment must be driven by the purpose of innovation in the
given social sectors in order to benefit from tax reductions.

To verify the status of innovative startups with social goals, the Law has
established a specific classification and monitoring procedure. Startups
with social goals must issue annual reports describing the social impact of
their operations, in accordance with Economic Development Ministry Circular no. 3677/C of 20 January 2015. The legal representative of the ISSGs
must issue a signed declaration confirming:

• that the company operates exclusively in one of the legally permitted
sectors;

• that the company's operations in this sector/these sectors is in the interest of the public good;

• that he undertakes to provide proof of the social impact generated.

All ISSGs must therefore issue the legally required document to guide
the process by which they identify, calculate and monitor their social impact.

In addition to the incentives and fiscal benefits available to all ISSG for
their first five years in business, the law provides additional advantages for
those with a social goal. These incentives are conditional on the annual
measurement and reporting of social impact (SI) in the form of a specific
document enclosed with the financial statements and available to stakeholders. The law therefore requires social dimension performance to be
measured in order to fulfil the criteria of transparency and the general
availability of information.

These additional criteria, specific to the social goal, underline the need to measure the business's social performance in the same way as its financial performance, combining the rewards of its social and economic patterns. Furthermore, operating in the specific social sectors generates particular market opportunities that tend to be hybrids between traditional economic opportunities and those open to conventional non-profit organizations, or in sectors where the demand for public goods is usually satisfied.

Figure 14. The social and economic dimensions in ISSG.

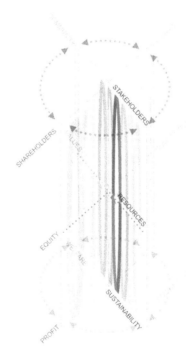

As a result of all the specific drivers of ISSGs, their social and economic configuration consists of synergic patterns that involve all their components (parties – contributions – rewards) and in which the two dimensions tend to merge.

4.5. Models and tools for measuring the social dimensions of ISSG

To aid in fulfilment of the reporting obligations established for these new hybrid firms, the Government has published a "Guide to the Drafting of

Social Impact Reports" which includes an example of how to calculate Social Return on Investment (SROI).

The guide provided by the law is not actually amongst the models considered and highlighted in our review of the literature, but it refers to SROI as the basis for quantitative measurement. As a result, for the analysis of the measurement of social dimension performance, ISSGs refer to SROI calculation.

The contents of the 30 retrieved documents [18] were analysed on the basis of several criteria and grouped under the main areas suggested by the guidelines and model adopted for the measurement and description of SI. C analysis is widely used in studies that analyse the firms' reporting documents (Krippendorf 1980). In particular, this methodology has produced important inputs for the study of stakeholder theory and social, environmental and intellectual capital reporting (Guthrie et al., 2004; Beattie and Thomson, 2007). The analysis was performed manually by three people and randomly checked for accuracy.

Five main areas of contents are identified on the basis of the SI guidelines provided by the law: main references to legislation and SROI calculation, output, outcome, and feedback description, stakeholder engagement, information disclosure and auditing of information. The information's presence was assessed considering the section in which it was placed, its quality, the level of coverage and its coherence with the definition offered by the guidelines. All the data collected were codified by items and then entered in the above tables. SROI calculation was analysed on a process-oriented basis.

The Italian guidelines for social impact measurement for ISSGs are based on the following assumption: "… Describing an organization's SI means assigning broader, longer-term effects to its business, in the sense of potential benefits or changes which its operations generate within the community in terms of knowledge, attitudes, state, quality of life and values. At the same time, these results must be converted into measurable terms …".

---

[18] The sample consists of thirty social impact reports obtained from one hundred and eighteen firms registered as ISSG at the end of 2016 (many of them were newly incorporated and their first financial statements were not available). The sample is representative of the different sectors in which these organisations are legally permitted to operate and covers the whole of the country. The Social Impact Reporting documents must be enclosed with the financial statements and lodged with the Chamber of Commerce.

Figure 15. The rewards of ISSG patterns.

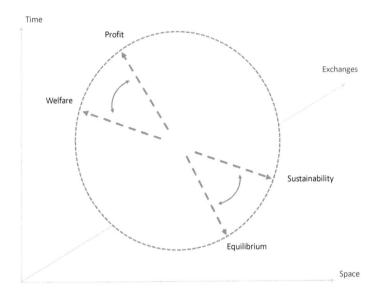

The main themes recommended by the guidelines are found in the various sections of a large proportion of the documents analysed, but the degree of detail provided varies significantly. Most information is provided, and in the greatest detail, in the section relating to social objectives, since this is the defining criterion of the ISSG itself and thus vital for its entitlement to the associated benefits.

The section with least coverage relates to the description of the process used for measuring SI, fundamental for its quantitative assessment. This section is actually completely missing in 8 documents out of 30. Moreover, even when this section contains a full description of the process, it does not always offer an SROI ratio calculation. In fact, analysing the quantitative aspect of the documents, in those cases when a section providing a quantitative measurement of the activities undertaken is included, the SROI is only calculated in 7 out of 30 documents.

In the section dedicated to the creation and measurement of social impact, documents should describe the drivers of value creation and detail the results achieved by the ISSG's activities. The analysis reveals that most information is qualitative: the content examined concentrates mostly on a description of the individual projects undertaken (provided in almost all the documents) and above all on the results produced by the single activities for the relevant stakeholders (87% of cases). This demonstrates consistency with the first phase of the reporting process, which defines the coordinates of the SI by detailing the mission and identifying the stakehold-ers. However, the latters' level of effective engagement upstream (involve-ment in the definition of the social objectives) and downstream (for valida-tion of the results achieved and other feedbacks) is unclear. Moreover, the fact that virtually none of these documents is published on the startups' web pages further underlines the lack of dialogue within the social dimen-sion patterns of the relevant stakeholders and communities. This confirms serious shortcomings in the third step of the accounting process, that of ex-ternal reporting.

When the measurement model examined does fulfil its function of de-scribing activities undertaken in order to achieve social objectives, no in-formation concerning the planning and management of these activities is provided. This observation is confirmed by the lack of performance indica-tors and a perspective approach to the results measured and points to the absence of the main elements of the last step in the social accounting pro-cess – managing and controlling. It is thus clear that this ISSFG social ac-counting processes is intended mainly for external communication and specially to comply with regulatory requirements.

4.6. Conclusions

The analysis of the data enables the identification of the main characteris-tics of the ISSGs social dimension's configuration and measures. The social accounting process analysed is not complete and as a consequence is not able to provide useful information for the assessment of the activities car-ried out by the ISSGs and how they fulfil their social goal stated in the mis-sion. It seems that this process is mainly oriented to pursue the normative requests: in fact, the social objectives are clearly identified and reported in all documents. This is consistent with the purposes of the measurement process in the case of ISSGs but it should be linked to the other phases of the accounting process and in particular it should be matched with the planning and controlling phase in order to bring behaviours in line with the ISSG's overall objectives placed in the configuration of its social and eco-nomic patterns.

The complexity and the importance of the accountability issues affect the efficiency of the measurement models that social enterprises adopt for assessing and communicating their social impact to multiple stakeholders. In the case of ISSG analysed, at the stage, it is not possible to pinpoint one-size-fits-all model even for this specific form of social enterprise.

Referring to the multidimensional patterns composed by long-term ex-pectations (outcomes and impacts), a Social Impact Plan that considers the gaps of the social impact measurement in the ISSGs can be a useful tool for assessing further the models and processes adopted. Setting out not only the social objectives but also the plan of the sequence of activities associated to the patterns of each dimension, can enact the missing phases of the social account processes progressively to the development of the stratups. This approach may solve also the problem that especially small and new social oriented organizations may encounter, in terms of complexity of accountability process, as it can be set out from the beginning of the firm's activities and applied for a long period that goes beyond a single year.

Chapter 5
BENEFIT CORPORATIONS

SUMMARY: 5.1. Benefit Corporations: an innovative configuration of firms' social and economic dimensions. – 5.2. Italian Benefit Corporations. – 5.3. The configuration of Benefit Corporations' social and economic dimensions. – 5.4. The accountability of B Corps: the B Impact Assessment. – 5.4.1. Economic and Social Impact. – 5.5. Conclusions.

5.1. Benefit Corporations: an innovative configuration of firms' social and economic dimensions

There are many types of companies which have developed in different economic and cultural contexts, registered under different statuses and laws, but in this case, the Benefit Corporation or Certified B Corps represents a common, international way of doing business, equivalent all over the world.

B Corps are one of the results of the re-evaluation of the concept of conventional for-profit business, taking into consideration the generation of wealth that businesses can produce for people and the environment protection they can provide. The new vision outlined by the CSR and sustainability movement provides the core values of Certified B Corps and Benefit Corporations, which represent a new form of corporate governance, focused on nurturing the sustainability approach.

Certified B Corps are "[…] companies based on how they create value for non-shareholding stakeholders, such as their employees, the local community, and the environment. Once a firm crosses a certain performance threshold on these dimensions, it makes amendments to its corporate charter to incorporate the interests of all stakeholders into the fiduciary duties of directors and officers. These steps demonstrate that a firm is following a fundamentally different governance philosophy than a traditional shareholder-centred corporation"[1].

Although B Corps are associated with Benefit Corporations, they may represent some "formal" differences. On the one hand, in many countries almost every company can change its legal structure to become a Benefit Corporation, a corporate form that requires for-profit companies to consider society and the environment alongside profit when they make deci-

---

[1] Kim S., Karlesky M., Myers C., Schifeling T., *Why Companies Are Becoming B Corporations*, Harvard Business Review Digital Articles [serial online]. June 17, 2016; 2-5. Available from: Business Source Complete, Ipswich, MA. Accessed December 21, 2017.

sions. On the other hand, a firm can become a Certified B Corp if it meets specific standards of accountability and transparency set out by B Lab [2].

More precisely "... B Corps are for-profit companies certified by the non-profit organization called B Lab [3] to meet rigorous standards of social and environmental performance, accountability, and transparency. Today, there is a growing community of more than 1,600 Certified B Corps from 42 countries and over 120 industries working together toward one unifying goal: to redefine success in business ..." [4]. As the B Lab statement makes clear, B Corps have been and are still rapidly expanding as a new form of business worldwide. Companies can choose to become one or both of these types of organization, and some well-known businesses have checked both boxes, including King Arthur Flour, Ben & Jerry's, Fratelli Carli and Patagonia.

Benefit Corporations are a type of corporation: they have an incorporating structure similar to conventional firms and to become one, a company must ensure that its articles of incorporation require the inclusion of all stakeholders, not only the financial community. Hence, Benefit Corporations represent a new model where there is a shift from a shareholder form to a stakeholder approach.

Figure 16. To B or not to B Corp: the path towards Benefit Corporations.

[2] Segarra M.B., Prepared. Cfo [serial online]. April 2014, 30(3):42-45, Available from: Business Source Complete, Ipswich, MA. Accessed December 21, 2017.

[3] "B Lab is a nonprofit organization that serves a global movement of people using business as a force for good. Its vision is that one day all companies compete not only to be the best in the world, but the Best for the World® and as a result society will enjoy a more shared and durable prosperity". Available online at https://www.bcorporation.net/what-are B Corps/about-b-lab, accessed on November 28, 2017.

[4] Available online at https://www.bcorporation.net/what-are-b-corps, accessed on November 28, 2017.

Furthermore, Benefit Corporations have the obligation to self-report on environmental and social impact on a yearly basis and voluntarily meet the standards they have set in their articles of association. Unlike B Corps, a Benefit Corporation is free to choose whatever assessment tool it wants to report the business's impact and it is not obliged to use the B Impact Assessment tool.

On the other hand, Certified B Corporations (also known as B Corporations or B Corps) are not necessarily Benefit Corporations but can be companies that have obtained certification under the B-Lab scheme, a certification or assessment tool that can be compared to others such as LEED certification or the Fair Trade label. Certified B Corps have similar accountability requirements to Benefit Corporations, but have some differences, one of which is the fact that they have to achieve a minimum score of 80/200 in their Impact Assessment and issue a re-assessment report every two years. Furthermore, they have to pay a membership fee based on their yearly revenue, which Benefit Corporations do not have to pay. These fees go to support the non-profit activities of B Lab and grant the company membership benefits, such as being part of the B Corp community, a community of Certified B Corp companies that support each other financially.

The following table summarizes the main differences between Benefit Corporations and B Corps:

Table 3. Benefit Corporations vs Certified B Corps.

	Structure	Social and Environmental Performance	Assessment tool
Benefit Corporations	It is a type of company. The B Corp model is incorporated in the company's business.	Yearly self-reporting	All
Certified B Corps	Are not necessarily Benefit Corporations, but obtained the B Lab certification.	Have to issue a report every year and score minimum 80/200 (re-assessment every two year)	Only B Lab

In the light of these considerations, both Benefit Corporations and B Corps can be described as a new, innovative and cutting-edge form of business, developing worldwide thanks to a common, international standard set of articles of association that permits easy comparison especially among B Corps from all over the world: "B Corps are a new type of company that uses the power of business to solve social and environmental problems" [5] . Being a Certified B Corp or a Benefit Corporation reflects the image of a company that chooses to prioritize societal and environmental agendas by seeking profit on a long-term scale, and represents the solution to a way of doing business that is no longer sustainable. Furthermore, business has been re-evaluated as a way of helping societies, and providing services and aid which some states and national governments appear to be having difficulty in supplying. As inequality is rising even in advanced societies, Benefit Corporations and Certified B Corps are seen by many governments as a mean of helping to fill this gap. The focus is on a new category of entrepreneurs who are not doing charity, but on the contrary are generating profits through the traditional model of profit making enterprises and at the same time solving the world's social issues by stimulating new markets, creating jobs and helping markets, which are apparently falling short in generating wealth and distributing it to their societies.

These companies' innovative aspects lie not only in their principles and the scheme's worldwide scale of action but also in the fact that companies of any size and from any business sector can become a Benefit Corporation or Certified B Corp. In fact, as stated on B Lab's website, which provides clear information on the world's Benefit Corporations and Certified B Corps, the sectors in which this business model operates are variegated.

The majority of Benefit Corporations and Certified B Lab businesses are small and medium sized enterprises (SMEs) and start-ups. The reason why more companies this size become B Corps or obtain the B Lab certification than big multinational firms is because of the business's legal nature; SMEs can easily incorporate new practices and bylaws and, given their modest size, they also do not encounter many difficulties when it comes to reporting their footprint, whereas big companies and corporations would require more time. On the other hand, bigger businesses and corporations still seem to find the challenge of becoming Certified B Corps too great. The reason behind this lies in the complexity of their corporate legal structures, especially for corporations that have subsidiaries around the world.

However, company size does not totally preclude a business from becoming a Benefit Corporation or Certified B Corp: from private to public, with or without subsidiaries, all kinds of businesses can "B the change" [6]. If

---

[5] Graham-Nye J., B Corporations: *A New Kind of Company Needing a New Kind of Funding Model*, Huffington Post, April 30, 2015, available online at http://www.huffing tonpost.com/jason-grahamnye/BCorporations-a-new-kind_b_7174520.html, accessed on November 28, 2017.

[6] "B the change" is a commonly used expression of B Lab, https://www.bcorpora tion.net/b-the-change, accessed on November 29, 2017.

the parent company decides to become a Benefit Corporation, all its subsidiaries must convert as well. Despite the major difficulties, there are multinational corporations, with annual revenues worth billions of dollars, which have obtained B Lab certification, such as Natura Cosmèticos and Triodos Bank. On the other hand, if a parent company does not choose to become a B Corp, its subsidiaries and certified brands may still choose to obtain this certification.

Despite these difficulties, B Lab is committed to expanding and to assisting multinational companies to obtain their certification: to do this, it has established the Multinationals and Public Markets Advisory Council (MPMAC) with the aim of addressing the possible legal and institutional issues that might keep these companies from changing their corporate structure or meeting the requirement for this certification.

5.2. Italian Benefit Corporations

As Benefit Corporations have been gradually introduced into each country's economic system at different times, it is interesting to focus on the Italian case, since Italy was the world's second country, after the United States, to introduce this new form of business, on December 1, 2016, and ever since it has experienced extraordinary growth in the number of companies that have changed their status to become Benefit Corporations – "Società Benefit" (at the end of 2017, more than 100 firms were registered as Benefit Corporations under Italian law [7]).

Among the numerous European countries in which the B Corp movement has taken hold, Italy was the first in Europe and second in the world, after the USA, to approve a law for this new legal form, inspiring many other countries. The law in question is Decree Law no.1882 of 17/04/2015 on Benefit Corporations and the statutory regulation is Law no. 208, Paragraphs 376-384, incorporated in the 2016 Budget Law and published in the Italian Official Journal on December 28, 2015. As the numbers show, the B Corporation movement is particularly significant: on December 31, 2016, 64 companies were already registered as B Corporations as defined by Italian law, of which 60% were companies with minimal share capital, while the others varied across a wide range, from non-profit to commercial companies (Maccaferri, 2016).

The law lists all the characteristics of this new type of firm in detail, in-

---

[7] There doesn't exists an official register of Benefit Corporations till now in Italy but Benefit Corporations can voluntarily register themselves online at www.societabenefit.net. A list of registered Benefit Corporation is accessible to the public.

cluding the purpose, description of the structure, legal aspects, obligations, responsibilities, impact assessment and management control processes of the Benefit Corporation. The purposes of shared benefits should be specifically indicated in the Benefit Corporation's corporate purpose and are pursued through management processes aimed at balancing shareholders' expectations with those of the stakeholders on whom the economic activity may have an impact. Companies other than benefit corporations that intend to pursue purposes of common benefit are required to amend the articles of their Deed of Incorporation and Articles of Association, in compliance with the relative rules, and these changes are filed, registered and published in accordance with the provisions for each type of company. Benefit Corporations are permitted to add the words Benefit Corporation – "Società Benefit", or their abbreviation to their name and to use this denomination in securities issued, in documentation and in communications with third parties[8]. The company is obliged to prepare an annual report on the pursuit of common benefit, to be annexed to the normal corporate financial statements. This report is fundamental: it should include the description of the specific objectives, the methods and actions implemented by the board of directors for the pursuit of the specific common benefit objectives and any circumstances that have prevented or slowed down their achievement, the impact assessment generated using an external evaluation standard that contains specific evaluation areas and, finally, a section that describes the future objectives that the company intends to pursue in the following year.

Specifically, the external evaluation standard used by the Benefit Corporation must be comprehensive and appropriately structured to assess the impact of the company and its actions in pursuing the aim of shared benefits for people, communities, territories and the environment, cultural and social assets and programmes, public bodies and associations and other stakeholders, and must be drawn up by an organization not controlled by or connected to the Benefit Corporation. It should be credible, because it is developed by an institution that has the necessary social and environmental impact assessment skills, and transparent, because information about it is in the public domain. The impact produced should be analysed and evaluated in four areas: corporate governance, workers, other stakeholders and the environment[9].

However, the Italian case does present some problems regarding the

---

[8] DDL 1882 del 2015, "Disposizioni per la diffusione di società che perseguono il duplice scopo di lucro e di beneficio comune", pp. 3-7.

[9] DDL 1882 del 2015, "Disposizioni per la diffusione di società che perseguono il duplice scopo di lucro e di beneficio comune", Allegato A (articolo 2, comma 1, lettera c).

correct implementation of this new form of business: for example, Italian B Corporation legislation seems lacking in rules to regulate transparency and reporting standards. Furthermore, Decree Law no. 1882 of April 17, 2015 still seems to be vague when it comes to which companies can become B Corporations and most cases are left open to interpretation. According to the aforementioned law, all types of companies covered by the Italian Civil Code can become a B Corporation. However, it fails to issue any provisions regarding the transition to B Corporations for Joint Ventures, Social Cooperatives, Social Enterprises and Innovative Startups. With regard to Joint Ventures and Innovative Startups, there are no specific provisions that regulate their possible change of status to become B Corps, but since they are for-profit organizations, there is no reason why they cannot acquire the status of B Corporations. On the other hand, Social Businesses encounter an obstacle when it comes to their articles of association, since their non-profit nature is incompatible with the for-profit character of the B Corps. However, there is nothing to prevent these businesses from changing their status to for-profit organizations and subsequently becoming B Corps.

After illustrating what a B Corporation, or B Corp is, and after providing an example of its local nature, it is time to focus on particular features and data to demonstrate this new form of business's usefulness to society in practical terms, through the configuration of its patterns and the social impact produced. The following sections of this chapter will therefore focus on a small sample of 12 Italian Benefit Corporations that are also B Corps[10], analysing them through their financial statement data and B Impact Assessment, with the aim of identifying the distinctive features or common characteristics of these companies' social and economic patterns. In the awareness that studies of Benefit Corporation are still in their infancy and there is a shortage of sources, studies and materials, this study aims to find interesting insights for future analysis, when Benefit Corporations are much more widespread and the abundance of cases, sources, literature and studies allows a more detailed empirical analysis. It is still early days to demonstrate, theorize and measure their social dimension, but all the same we have identified some interesting data, worth examining to identify possible paths for future studies.

---

[10] After explaining the differences between Benefit Corporation and B Corps, from now the terms will be used interchangeably, to describe measures and reports with a focus on firms' social dimension assessment.

5.3. The configuration of Benefit Corporations' social and economic dimensions

The value of meeting the legal requirement for Benefit Corporation and B Corp certification is that it bakes sustainability into the DNA of the company as it grows, attracts capitals, or plans succession, ensuring that the firm's mission can better survive new management, new investors, or even new ownership.

The aim of producing a positive impact for society and the environment is translated into concrete "sustainable objectives" that are integrated into Benefit Corporations' core business, as economic success is closely linked to both their environmental and social performance. It is important to understand how these organizations combine different logics – the market logic and social ones – because their definition and performance arises from the hybridity of their performance in the social and economic dimensions. A B Corp sees profit as a means of achieving its social and environmental goals and growing profits can mean a greater impact through an enhanced "give back" sequence.

More in detail, the distinctive features of a Benefit Corporation could be defined in this way:

1. the company's objective of creating a positive material impact on society and the environment;

2. the expansion of the obligations and responsibilities of the directors, to take into account other interests – environmental, social and other stakeholders – as well as the financial interests of its shareholders;

3. the obligation to provide an annual report on social and environmental performance using a comprehensible, credible, independent and transparent third-party standard.

Regarding the first point, it is important to underline that B Corps are obliged to pursue the objective of creating "general public benefit" and may identify one or more "specific public benefit objectives". This differentiates them from normal companies, which are allowed to formulate any objective, without explicit obligations in these terms. The distinction between general public benefit and specific public benefit highlights a peculiarity of Benefit Corporations. The purpose of creating this new type of company is to establish a new type of firm that voluntarily adopts the objective of benefiting society and the environment in general, as well as shareholders. Entrepreneurs, investors and consumers interested in reducing polluting emissions may not be interested in reducing waste, or may wish to reduce both, while remaining indifferent to creating economic opportunities for low-income individuals or disadvantaged social communities. The B Corp's business model is able to give these entrepreneurs and investors the flexibility and protection to pursue each of these specific public benefits, working, in each case, to a common public benefit goal. This ensures that the Benefit Corporation can pursue any specific common benefit target, but overall work for a general public benefit [11]. Therefore, it is important that the company first of all has a general objective of public benefit; it will be its task to express it in many specific objectives, depending on its core business and characteristic patterns. This locates the social and economic dimensions patterns more specifically, since they should be considered in strict relation to the specific objectives set up by the Benefit Corporation's management processes, not only in terms of rewards but also with regard to resources.

Another fundamental factor for the correct functioning of this innovative business model is the fact that directors' obligations and responsibilities are extended to include other interests, in addition to the financial interests of shareholders. The Benefit Corporation also expands the obligations and responsibilities of the board of directors to the pursuit of social and environmental objectives, enabling managers to pursue goals of common benefit without fear of defaulting, free from the yoke of profit maximization. Because they are called upon to respond to these social and environmental goals, they are no longer forced to put profit before other goals in companies' decision-making processes. This means that pattern management should consider the use of both social and economic resources for the pursuit of profit– and mission-driven activities. The traditional economic rewards shift closer to social ones, integrating the two components for all patterns referring to the parties in a traditional firm (Figure 17).

---

[11] Examples of specific public benefits were elaborated in the case of the State of California, which has drawn up a non-exhaustive list of seven possibilities: Targeting products or services that benefit individuals - or communities - from low-income or disadvantaged backgrounds; Promoting economic opportunities for individuals or communities beyond the ordinary job creation in the natural course of business; Preserving the environment; Improving human health; To promote the arts, the sciences and the diffusion of knowledge; To increase the flow of capital to entities with a public benefit objective, The realization of any other particular benefit for society or the environment.

Figure 17. The rewards of Benefit Corporations' patterns.

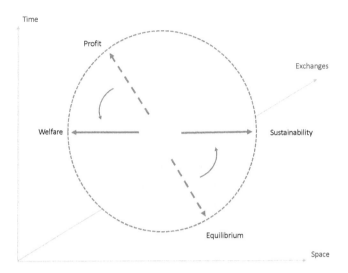

In fact, the categories of patterns made up of shareholders and stakeholders maintain their distinctive roles; communities and markets remain separate providers of social and economic categories of opportunities and responsibilities, managed and measured through processes that feed each other. As a result, the configuration of Benefit Corporations' social and economic dimensions differs from that of ordinary businesses, as the economic and social rewards are very close to each other and resources are managed in an integrated way (as shown in Figure 18), but also it differs from the ISSG configuration earlier, as the parties conserve their distinctive roles and create different patterns even though their expectations and rewards change compared to those of a traditional business.

Figure 18. The social and economic dimensions in Benefit Corporations.

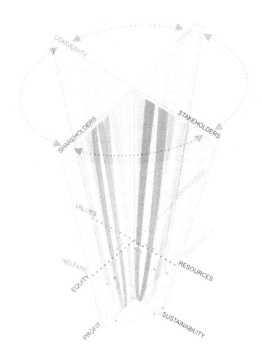

The third important feature of this business model is precisely the obligation to produce a report on its social and environmental performance, through a reliable third-party standard. It is mandatory to produce a report on the benefits their performance has brought for all stakeholders each year, and make it available to the public on the company website. While financial results can be measured through traditional financial statements and other widely used tools, there is still no predefined standard for Benefit Corporations' measurements of social and environmental performance. Each company is free to choose the standard it decides to use, provided that it respects the obligations of credibility, independence, comprehensibility and transparency.

5.4. The accountability of B Corps: the B Impact Assessment

Identification of a group of companies suitable for analysis started from the official Benefit Corporation website, selecting companies that were both Benefit Corporations and B Corps. From this group, by analysing the individual companies it was possible to identify the names of all the Italian B Corps operating in the "Food & Beverage" and "Services" sectors. The two sub-groups thus obtained were also checked at the business code level, to verify that they belonged to the same macro-sectors. Each company's B Impact Assessment was also retrieved from the B Lab webpage.

Starting from the balance sheet data, the values analysed (labour cost per employee and value added per employee) were calculated and reported for each of the companies. The results obtained were compared with the national average of the relative sectors, available in the Italian Institute of Statistics document: "Report on the competitiveness of the productive sectors – 2017 Edition". Finally, the data obtained from the comparison between the companies' financial statements and the industry averages were compared with the B Impact Assessments, with the aim of observing similar trends and checking for any relationship between the two performances.

It is clear that, given the narrowness of the sample of companies on which it was possible to work – due to the fact that there are still very few Benefit Corporations in Italy – the analysis carried out should not be considered as generating certain, incontrovertible results. A work on a sample of 12 companies cannot pretend to definitively identify common features for all the B Corps on the Italian market. However, given the novelty of the context, any result that this study is able to provide will be considered as a starting point on which to base future analyses, in the awareness that any such results could equally well be valuable clues or misleading results, due to the peculiarity of the few companies examined and the small scale of the sample.

To obtain certification, a Benefit Corporation must undergo the "B Impact Assessment" and obtain a minimum of 80 points out of the 200 available. The B Impact Assessment issued by B Lab has evolved over the years and is renewed more or less every two years. Five versions have been published since 2007, with the most recent version published in 2016. The B Impact Assessment has impressive origins: it was built by B Lab taking into account the work on impact measurement conducted by several organizations and companies over the last few decades, including GRI, Wiser Earth, other specific certifications (Fair Trade, Organic, ISO, 1% For the Planet) and corporate best practices. A variety of ideas with a single common purpose: to give companies the opportunity to measure and manage the social and environmental impact of their business on all stakeholders, thanks to a standardized and easy-to-use framework.

In 2015, a shorter version named "Quick Impact Assessment" was launched for companies measuring their social impact for the first time. It varies from the B Impact Assessment in significant respects: it contains 20-30 questions (instead of 50-150), it takes on average 20 minutes to complete (against the 90 minutes of the B Impact Assessment), and it does not return an "overall" score, like the normal test, but provides the companies that fill in the test with a benchmark for specific questions. It is not sufficient for the award of Benefit Corporation certification, but it is a useful tool for companies attempting to measure their social and environmental impact for the first time and can help them to understand on which areas they need to improve their social dimension activities.

The questionnaire is divided into four macro-areas: Environment, Governance, Workers, and Community. For each of these sections, a score is given for the social impact measured in the specific field: the sum of these scores constitutes the overall score.

However, there is not just one single version of the B Impact Assessment – the evaluation standard is available in 72 different versions, each different from the others in terms of size, geographical market and industry. It is very important to verify that a company answers the correct questionnaire, because the questions and scores may change from case to case on the basis of these specificities. When a company registers for the Assessment, it is asked to provide information on its size, market and industry. On the basis of the information related to these three fields, the one of the 72 possible combinations of the B Impact Assessment most suitable for the company's business is proposed for the measurement of its social and environmental impacts.

With regard to the size of the company, the framework takes into account the number of employees and divides companies into 6 groups: workers that are owners of the firm; 1-9 employees; 10-49 employees; 50-250 employees; 250-1000 employees; and 1000-10000 employees. Analyzing the market where the firm operates, the B Impact Assessment version changes depending on whether the company is operating in Developed Markets, US and Global (DM) or Emerging Markets (EM). Finally, the Industry-related variables are divided into four categories, based on the areas in which the company operates: Manufacturing; Service; Wholesale; Agriculture.

Given these main drivers of the firm's economic dimension, the customizability of the standard allows a targeted, effective and "tailor-made" assessment of firms' social dimension patterns. A consulting company with only one employee will have a set of questions on the Environment section that is definitely different from a clothing manufacturing with two production plants. A company's environmental impact changes radically depending on whether it is a US steel company with 500 employees or an Indian service company with 4 employees. The social impact produced on workers, communities and the environment takes into account the conditions (geographical, political and social) of these areas, which is why a score can be significant in one region – or in a specific industry – and only conventional in the others.

This characteristic of the B Corps' measuring process, perfectly fits with the first step of data gathering and the "who, what and how" needs of the accounting data specified in the social accounting process proposed in the previous chapter.

Analysing each measurement area, the governance section examines the company's organizational behaviour, with questions mainly on corporate accountability (corporate mission, code of ethics, board of directors, Key Performance Indicators), transparency (financial control, annual report, annual feedback) and "governance metrics" (focus on the last fiscal year and revenues). The company is asked a series of questions on its corporate governance and its formal commitment – for example, if it has signed a contract or there is a resolution of the board of directors to adopt a legal formula that takes into consideration the community, the environment and stakeholders. In general, the purpose of this section is to understand the extent to which the company has formal, operational mechanisms with regard to its positive social impact: a mission, specific bodies, procedures and best practices. It is important that the commitment is formalized and public and supported by an appropriate structure, since otherwise there is a risk of only reporting good intentions, never formalized or implemented.

The Workers section examines the company's positive impact on its employees. The Workers area is in turn divided into various sections:

• Workers Metrics – investigates the types of contract with which employees are hired;

• Compensation and Benefits – mainly analyzes the differences between the firm's minimum wage and the average living wage and the bonuses offered to employees. The metrics also consider the benefits offered to workers: health care plan, dental check-ups, life insurance, short-term disability, long-term disability, paid leave days, maternity or paternity leave, early retirement, etc.;

• Employee Training – What training is offered? Does training go beyond normal work training, teaching so-called life skills (personal financial planning, IT skills, language proficiency), etc.?;

• Employee Ownership – considers the percentage of full-time workers who own company shares or participate in an Employee Stock Ownership Plan, and the percentage of the company that is owned by the workers;

• Work Environment – analyses whether there is a formalized process that allows employees to freely express their feedbacks, flexible working options, the company policy in terms of health and safety, etc.

The Community section considers issues concerning the community within which the firm operates, such as job creation, diversity, civic engagement and giving, local involvement, suppliers, distributors and products. Some of the metrics considered are:

• job creation – such as the number of full-time and part-time workers who have been hired;
• diversity – the percentage of the members of the board of directors, or other corporate governance bodies, who are women, or persons that belong to low income communities or to other unrepresented groups (minorities, people with disabilities, etc.);
• civic engagement and giving – the percentage of profit or sales was donated to charity by the company;
• suppliers, distributors and products – percentage of products and materials purchased that have certification or social/environmental approval from independent third parties.

The Environment area analyses the business's impact on the environment and the firm's efforts to preserve the natural environment through the management of its properties. In particular, the analysis focuses on how energy is used (Energy Use), on plants and all the problems related to them in terms of waste and pollution (Facilities), on suppliers and raw materials in the production chain (Supply Chain) and on the actual production process, analysing the consequences and the impact on the environment (Manufacturing). For example, in the "Transportation, Distribution and Suppliers" section, companies are asked to provide details on the pollutant emissions of their shipments, the use of chemical products in their supply chain and the "green" practices of their suppliers. The "Inputs" section analyses the saving and conservation of energy, water and other materials in the company's operations. As for raw materials, companies are evaluated on their use of energy and renewable sources, on the packaging of raw materials and the relative pollution/waste, on the Life Cycle Assessment (LCA) – a tool to evaluate the interactions of a product/service with the environment taking into account its whole life cycle – and finally on the use of water. With regard to finished products, the company is required to report on issues such as polluting emissions, hazardous waste and waste of water. Detailed data is then requested on air quality, on the recycling processes of raw materials, and on the "environmental" quality of buildings and company premises. One example of data required on these issues concerns company programmes for the recovery and recycling of materials such as paper, cardboard, plastic, glass and metal, compostable waste and so on.

Some versions of the B Impact Assessment also include a Customers section, aimed at measuring the impact the company on its customers. The section seeks to understand whether the company sells a product or service that generates a public benefit, and whether these products or services have benefited disadvantaged and "unserved" populations or social communities. The data in this section is therefore intended to measure whether the product or service offered by the company is designed to solve a social or environmental problem: improving health, preserving the environment, creating economic opportunities for individuals or communities, or promoting arts and sciences.

This phase of B Impact Assessment, providing specific metrics for each category of social and Environmental issues, corresponds to the second step of the social accounting process, "Data Evaluation", making use of different models' quantifications techniques (such as GRI, Full Costing, etc.)

Finally, the Impact Business Models section aims to identify the business models focused on the environment and social impact best suited to the firm's core business. A business model can have a significant direct impact, simply by reason of the product/service that the company markets: some products have a positive (social) impact on communities, customers and the environment. For companies that do not deal with products of this kind, there are other business models that can make a positive social impact: for example, by identifying and serving disadvantaged communities and involving them in the firm's processes as customers, workers, or suppliers. In this way, the company produces a positive social impact on a socially disadvantaged community through the construction of its business model. Finally, another positive business model that companies can adopt is the one that has the greatest social impact in the production chain: suppliers, distributors and customers are part of the firm's virtuous commitment and contribute to achieving a positive social performance.

The information provided and analysed in this section can give important indications on the management system that companies can adopt in order to integrate their way of being a "benefit" for the community and the environment. When this information also considers and sets future objectives, it can completely represent the fourth step of the social accounting process, "Management and Control".

The B Impact Assessment allows companies to compare their performance with the average of ordinary companies, with the average of the companies involved in Sustainability and with the B Corp average. The comparison is extended to the overall score and to the individual Areas and Categories. The possibility of this direct comparison is a great opportunity for firms: apart from the information provided by the global score, they are able to understand which social dimension areas need improvement and which already produce excellent results. A company with a global score of 115 (sufficient for certification) will be aware it will have a few issues in need of improvement: through access to this type of information – the benchmark – it could find out that it has a lower performance compared to ordinary businesses in some areas (for example in local involvement), despite the overall score. The comparability of the B Impact Assessment allows companies to dig deeper into the global score and to identify – through benchmarking – the areas of social dimension that still offer room for improvement.

This representation of the mutual benefit information and the relative report, required by law in the case of Italian Benefit Corporations, can be considered consistent with the reporting steps found in every accounting process.

5.4.1. Economic and Social Impact

To take a different look at the impact produced by the Benefit Corporations, a comparison of some of the results obtained from the balance sheet statements and the B Impact Assessment will be presented. Given their shared objectives and the multidimensional rewards they should demonstrate, this analysis tries to investigate if there is an interaction between economic and social performance measurements. More in detail, the relationship between the "cost of labour per employee" deriving from the financial statements and the "compensation, benefits and training" item of the B Impact Assessment will be analysed. This last item, belonging to the Workers section of the B Impact Assessment, aims to investigate whether the company matches an appropriate salary with benefits, training and other bonuses equivalent to those that other employers can grant. The rewards in employee patterns are analysed in terms of salary and other benefits. Among all the items of the B Impact Assessment, this is the one that can be most clearly related to the labour cost per employee, although bearing in mind that it is not the same thing: the Assessment also takes qualitative data into account, while the balance sheet captures only quantitative figures. Therefore, for the companies considered, the B Impact Assessment scores reported for the "compensation, benefits and training" item was compared to the median score, or the average score, obtained in this particular item by all the companies that underwent the B Impact Assessment. The purpose of this investigation is to find out whether a positive performance in the comparison between balance sheet data and sector average is associated with a positive performance in the comparison between the B Impact Assessment item and the relative median score, and vice versa.

With regard to the "cost of labour per employee", in the Food and Beverage cluster, 3 out of 6 companies (50%) report values above the sector average indicated by Istat; in the Services cluster, there are 4 out of 6 companies with above-average values. Without taking into account the division into clusters, it can be noted that more than half of the B Corp study group (7 out of 12 companies) have a labour cost per employee above the average of their sector.

With regard to the "value added per employee" item, in the Food and Beverage cluster, 4 out of 6 companies show values above the industry average; in the Services cluster, on the other hand, 5 out of 6 companies show values above the industry average. Without taking the division into clusters into account, it can be seen that 9 out of 12 of the companies surveyed show values above the average of their sector for the "Value added per employee" productivity index.

In addition to the comparison between individual companies and industry averages, interesting data also emerge from the comparison between cluster and industry averages. The Food and Beverage cluster shows a labour cost per employee slightly lower than the sector average (-10%) – however this data could be polluted by the presence in the cluster of two wineries, which probably offer atypical results, compared with the Food industries sector – but an added value per employee significantly higher than the sector average (more than 30%). The Services cluster, on the other hand, portrays a virtuous B Corp group, with a labour cost per employee above the sector average (20% higher) and an added value per employee even further above the industry average (more than twice the industry average).

In the Food and Beverage cluster: companies with a labour cost per worker above the industry average also have a score higher than the median score for the compensation, benefits and training B Impact Assessment item. Similarly, only one case – with a labour cost per employee significantly lower than the industry average – is placed below the median score of the B Impact Assessment. The remaining two companies have a score of the B Impact Assessment close to the median score.

The Services cluster confirms, in part, the trends observed in the first group of companies. Three firms with a labour cost per employee much higher than the sector average were also well above the median score in the B Impact Assessment. The other three companies in the cluster have more unexpected results: the only company that has a higher labour cost per employee than the sector average achieves a score equal to the median score of the B Impact Assessment. It is worth pointing out that both scores are very close to the relative average values: this can be seen as an indication that there is some link between the two performances. The two remaining cases record excellent scores in the B Impact Assessment, but lower than average values for the labour cost per employee. Probably the difference is due to qualitative factors that the financial data cannot capture.

Looking at the companies without considering the clusters, we can observe some common tendencies: for 7 companies out of 12, there is a common trend between the two measurements – economic and social data. For a labour cost per employee above the industry average, a score in the "compensation, benefits and training" item is higher than the median score; at a lower value, it corresponds to a lower score. It is worth noting that these are also the largest companies in terms of the number of employees and therefore easier to measure than other companies with only a few employees, for which values may be affected by other features that have a much greater weight and may influence the average.

It can be hypothesized that, since the B Impact Assessment considers qualitative aspects that cannot be captured by the financial statement measurements, these companies actually have a very positive impact on employees even with a lower than average labour cost per employee. The "compensation, benefits and training" is not the direct counterpart of "cost of labour per employee", and the performances remind us of this fact.

5.5. Conclusions

With its strict guidelines and the holistic approach of the B lab report, B Lab certification helps to achieve sustainability and the fair distribution of profits, by ensuring that Benefit Corporations and certified B Corps companies are fully aligned with the configuration of their social and economic dimensions.

Thanks to the modification of the firm's articles of association and the responsibility placed on the board of directors for its social and environment issues, as well as its economic management, Benefit Corporations are able to figure out an appropriate configuration of patterns that incorporate both social and economic objectives and consider the impact of the business activities on all the parties involved.

Given that for a long time companies, through their operations, have been seen as one of the main causes of social and environmental problems such as pollution, waste, obesity and social disparity, and have therefore also been seen as responsible for solving them, Benefit Corporations try, through their own operations, to integrate social and economic issues by involving all their stakeholders and their respective contributions and rewards in the stakeholder-resources-rewards patterns they measure and manage. Instead of seeing them as a source of trade-offs, Benefit Corporations are committed to embedding these issues in their traditional measurement and management processes, based on the synergies of the patterns between the two dimensions. This integration emerges in particular from the detailed analysis performed by the B Impact Assessment. This tool allows measurement and investigation of the global impact of B Corps' specific business activities and identifies the synergies among the patterns, thus distinguishing the different areas where social and environmental impact occurs. Furthermore, the combination of B Impact Assessment and balance sheet data may give companies an effective, credible overview of their social and environmental performance in economic terms, and enable them to constantly monitor and manage the mutual influence that they may have on one-another. It is interesting to note that this integrated evaluation was confirmed in many of the B Corps examined: where the economic measurements of the social issues analyzed were above the industry average, these results were confirmed and often accompanied by positive social performance, analyzed in a similar area of the B Impact Assessment and above the sector benchmark data.

Chapter 6
FINAL CONSIDERATIONS

SUMMARY: 6.1. Final considerations.

6.1. Final considerations

Introduced as part of the 2030 Agenda for Sustainable Development, the 17 Sustainable Development Goals (SDG) present an opportunity for business-led solutions and technologies to be developed and implemented to address the world's biggest sustainable development challenges. This is a good time to analyze how companies have already embraced them and how their activities can further support the SDGs that can be aligned with their core business.

One of the first things that firms need to do is to work out how the SDGs fit in with their existing sustainability plans. The SDGs represent both a commitment to responsibility and sustainability for the business community, and a framework for the development of its activities.

This study focuses on how the numerous issues and challenges of CSR and Corporate Sustainability can significantly change the way business is developed, if the existing and potential opportunities and synergies between firms' social and economic dimensions are configured, seized and managed. Seizing these opportunities and synergies requires the enhancement and development of the multiple measurement techniques and tools that companies already use in their management activities.

Moving a step further, each company's social dimension can be defined within the configuration of stakeholders – resources – rewards patterns intrinsic to its interactions with its environment and embedded in its business activities. More specifically, the value proposition of the framework for analysis provided is: To provide a dynamic, synergic configuration of Parties – Contributions – Rewards patterns and the social and economic dimensions of firms which they constitute, contemplating the different phases of a firm's development, to allow the establishment of appropriate governance models, management processes and performance measurements. Based on this approach, the aim is to guide firms in identifying management activities grounded in and suited to their prevalent social and economic dimension patterns, in order to support current and future strategies and establish adequate measurement and communication tools for pursuing their mission.

The analysis of the framework reveals that the process of integrating and nurturing the exchanges between the economic and social dimensions, made up of stakeholder-contributions-rewards patterns, could potentially further develop existing governance models and produce outcomes with even greater potential, generating new opportunities for the growth of the firm's activities, as in the case of innovation and crisis management.

Multidimensional identification of patterns can offer a means of combining and leveraging actors' resources across both dimensions. This, in turn, offers opportunities for engaging these patterns in the growth of the firm's operations while promoting inclusive management models and creating new openings.

As the analysis of the multidimensional pattern configuration in the two types of firms studied indicates, patterns can help to identify outcomes of significance for both dimensions. In particular, in:

– Innovative Start-ups with a Social Goal, they can help to link market-driven activities and innovation processes, with inclusive social and economic impact generation;

– Benefit Corporations, they can foster interactions between profit-driven activities and firms' traditional activities, generating sustainable and equitable rewards.

They may facilitate cross-dimensional dialogue intended to align different actors and interests around common activities, potential synergies and collaboration. This, in turn, can enhance the effective use of all resources (economic, social and environmental) by reducing their waste, fragmentation and duplication – an increasing concern for both shareholders and stakeholders.

Furthermore, analyzing the similarities in the ways in which different patterns tend to identify, contribute to and evaluate the firm's activities can enhance the interactions between the two dimensions and increase the probability of developing synergies via positive collaborative processes and facilitating performance measurement and communication among them. The analysis of the principal social and environmental impact measurement and reporting models (i.e. Global Reporting Initiative, Social Return on Investments, Social Balanced Scorecard, etc.) and their main features was carried out with the aim of investigating their potential in this process of assessing and managing the social dimension, and tailoring their use more closely to the specific patterns to which they refer.

One important topic that should be considered for the better application of measurement tools and processes to the demand for accountability in relation to different forms of firms is stakeholder inclusiveness. The low incidence of stakeholder involvement in the cases of social accountability analyzed is confirmed by the lack of attention in social impact reports to the degree of inclusion of stakeholders and communities in this process (not covered at all in many cases). In fact, while in consolidated Corporate Social Responsibility reporting models stakeholder involvement is considered one of the pillars for both the definition of the materiality of social and environmental actions and the identification of the topics to be measured and reported, operative tools and mechanisms that consider the "dialogues" within firms' main patterns require further development in social accounting processes.

The framework and processes investigated can aid the identification, measurement and management of social dimension patterns and ease their integration into firms' operational and strategic decision-making, with the aim of assisting the mutual understanding and synergistic improvement of businesses' social, environmental and economic activities.

REFERENCES

AccountAbility, *AA1000APS AccountAbility Principles Standard*, London, UK, 2008.

AccountAbility, *AA1000AS Assurance Standard*, London, UK, 2008.

Ackoff R., *Redesigning the future*, John Wiley, New York, 1974.

Acquier A., Gand S., Szpirglas M., *From stakeholder to stakesholder management in crisis episodes: A case study in a public transportation company*, Journal of Contingencies and Crisis Management, 16(2), 101-114, 2008.

Adams C.A., *The ethical, social and environmental reporting – performance portrayal gap*, Accounting, Auditing and Accountability Journal, 17(5), 731-757, 2004.

Adams C.A., McNicholas P., *Making a difference: Sustainability reporting, accountability and organisational change*, Accounting, Auditing and Accountability Journal, 20(3), 382-402, 2007.

Agostinelli M., *Tempo e spazio nell'impresa postfordista*, Manifestolibri, Roma, 1997.

Aguilera R.V., Jackson G., *The cross-national diversity of corporate governance: Dimensions and determinants*, Academy of management Review, 28(3), 447-465, 2003.

Airoldi G., Amatori F., Invernizzi G., *Proprietà e Governo delle Aziende Italiane*, Egea, Milano, 1995.

Alpaslan C.M., Green S.E., Mitroff I.I., *Corporate governance in the context of crises: Towards a stakeholder theory of crisis management*, Journal of contingencies and crisis management, 17(1), 38-49, 2009.

Andorlini C., Ciappei C., *Imprenditorialità sociale tra sviluppo di comunità e creazione di valore*, Picini Editore, 2011.

Aoki, M., *Information, corporate governance and institutional diversity: Competitiveness in Japan, the USA, and the transitional economies*, Oxford University Press, Inc., 2000.

Aras G., Crowther D., *Governance and sustainability: An investigation into the relationship between corporate governance and corporate sustainability*, Management Decision, 46(3), 433-448, 2008.

Arvidson M., Lyon F., McKay S., Moro D., *Valuing the social? The nature and controversies of measuring social return on investment (SROI)*, Voluntary Sector Review, 4(1), 3-18, 2013.

Audia P.G., Freeman J., H., Reynolds, P.D., *Organizational foundings in community context: Instruments manufacturers and their interrelationship with other organizations*, Administrative Science Quarterly, 51(3), 381-419, 2006.

Augustine N.R., Sharma A., Kesner I.F., Smith N.C., Thomas R.J., Quelch J., ... Hill L., *Harvard business review on crisis management*, Harvard Business Press, 2000.

Ayuso S., Ángel Rodríguez M., García-Castro R., Ángel Ariño M., *Does stakeholder engagement promote sustainable innovation orientation?*, Industrial Management and Data Systems, 111(9), 1399-1417, 2011.

Bacq S., Janssen F., *The multiple faces of social entrepreneurship: A review of definitional issues based on geographical and thematic criteria*, Entrepreneurship and Regional Development, 23(5-6), 373-403, 2011.

Bagnoli L., Megali C., *Measuring performance in social enterprises*, Nonprofit and Voluntary Sector Quarterly, 40(1), 149-165, 2011.

Bailey D., Harte G., Sugden R., *Corporate disclosure and the deregulation of international investment*, Accounting, Auditing and Accountability Journal, 13(2), 197-218, 2000.

Battilana J., *Agency and institutions: The enabling role of individuals' social position*, Organization, 13(5), 653-676, 2006.

Beattie V., Thomson S. J., *Lifting the lid on the use of content analysis to investigate intellectual capital disclosures*, Accounting Forum, 31, (2), 129-163, 2007.

Bebbington J., Gray R., *Corporate accountability and the physical environment: social responsibility and accounting beyond profit*, Business Strategy and the Environment, 2(2), 1-11, 1993.

Bell S., Morse S., *Measuring sustainability: learning from doing*, Routledge, 2012.

Bengo I., Arena M., Azzone G., Calderini M., *Indicators and metrics for social business: a review of current approaches*, Journal of Social Entrepreneurship, 7(1), 1-24, 2015.

Berle A., Means G.C., *Private property and the modern corporation*, Comerce Clearing House, New York, 1932.

Berman S.L., Wicks A.C., Kotha S., Jones T.M., *Does stakeholder orientation matter? The relationship between stakeholder management models and firm financial performance*, Academy of Management journal, 42(5), 488-506, 1999.

Bertini U., *Il sistema d'azienda. Schema d'analisi*, Giappichelli, Torino, 1990.

Bhagat S., Jefferies R., *The Econometrics of Corporate Governance Studies*, Boston, MIT press, 2002.

Bocchi G., Ceruti M., *La sfida della complessità*, Mondadori, Milano, 2007.

Boje D.M., *Organizational change and global standardization: Solutions to standards and norms overwhelming organizations*, Routledge, 2015.

Borzaga C., Defourny J., *The emergence of social enterprise*, Vol. 4, Psychology Press. 2004.

Borzaga C., Fazzi L., *Governo e organizzazione per l'impresa sociale*, Roma, Carocci, 2008.

Boschee J., *Social entrepreneurship: The promise and the perils*, in Nicholls A., *Social entrepreneurship: New models of sustainable social change*, 356-390, 2006.

Brinckerhoff P.C., *Social entrepreneurship: The art of mission-based venture development*, John Wiley and Sons, 2000.

Bruni G., *Contabilità per l'alta direzione: il processo informativo funzionale alle decisioni di governo dell'impresa*, ETAS Libri, Milano, 1990.

Bruni G., *Le informazioni complementari al Bilancio. Quale reporting revolution?*, Rivista italiana di ragioneria e di economia aziendale, 1/2, 2007.

Bull M., *"Balance": the development of a social enterprise business performance analysis tool*, Social Enterprise Journal, 3(1), 49-66, 2007.
Burchell S., Clubb C., *Hopwood A. G., Accounting in its social context: Towards a history of value added in the United Kingdom*, Accounting, Organizations and Society, 10(4), 381-413, 1985.

Carroll A.B., Buchholtz A.K., *Business and society. Ethics and stakeholder management*, South-Western, Div. of Thomson Learning, New York, 2005.
Cattaneo M., *Principi di valutazione del capitale d'impresa*, Il Mulino, Bologna, 1998.
Catturi G., *Produrre e consumare, ma come*, Cedam, Padova, 1990.
Cerbioni F., Cinquini, L., Sòstero U., *Contabilità e bilancio*, Milan, McGraw-Hill, 2011.
Chandler Jr. A.D., *The visible hand: The managerial revolution in American business*, Harvard University Press, 1993.
Cheng M., Green W., Conradie P., Konishi N., Romi A., *The international integrated reporting framework: key issues and future research opportunities*, Journal of International Financial Management & Accounting, 25(1), 90-119, 2014.
Chirieleison C., *Le strategie sociali nel governo dell'azienda*, Giuffrè, Milano, 2002.
Chirieleison C., *Le strategie sociali nel governo dell'azienda*, Giuffrè, Milano, 2002.
Clarkson M.B.E., *A Stakeholder Framework for Analyzing and Evaluating Corporate Social Performance*, Academy of Management Review, 20(1), 92-117, 1995.
Clarkson M.E., *A stakeholder framework for analyzing and evaluating corporate social performance*, Academy of management review, 20(1), 92-117, 1995.
Coda V., *L'orientamento strategico dell'impresa*, Utet, Torino, 1988.
Coles J.W., McWilliams V.B., Sen N., *An examination of the relationship of governance mechanisms to performance*, Journal of management, 27(1), 23-50, 2001.
Connelly B.L., Certo S.T., Ireland R.D., Reutzel C.R., *Signaling theory: A review and assessment*, Journal of Management, 37(1), 39-67, 2011.
Coombs W.T., Holladay S.J., *The handbook of crisis communication*, (Vol. 22), John Wiley & Sons, 2011.
Cooper C., *The non and nom of accounting for (M)other Nature*, Accounting, Auditing and Accountability Journal, 5(3),16-39, 1992.
Cooper S.M., Owen D.L., *Corporate social reporting and stakeholder accountability: The missing link*, Accounting, Organizations and Society, 32(7), 649-667, 2007.
Corvi E., *La comunicazione aziendale. Obiettivi, tecniche, strumenti*, Egea, Milano, 2007.
Coupland C., *Corporate social and environmental responsibility in web-based reports: Currency in the banking sector?*, Critical perspectives on accounting, 17(7), 865-881, 2006.
Crane A., Glozer S., *Researching corporate social responsibility communication: Themes, opportunities and challenges*, Journal of Management Studies, 53(7), 1223-1252, 2016.
Crossan M.M., Apaydin M., *A multi-dimensional framework of organizational innovation: A systematic review of the literature*, Journal of management studies, 47(6), 1154-1191, 2010.

CSR Europe, Global Reporting Initiative (GRI), *Member State Implementation of Directive 2014/95/EU, A comprehensive overview of how Member States are implementing the EU Directive on Non-financial and Diversity Information*, 2017, accessed on 27 September 2017 at: https://www.csreurope.org/sites/default/files/uploads/CSR%20Europe_GRI%20NFR%20publication_0.pdf.

Dacin P.A., Dacin M.T., Matear M., *Social entrepreneurship: Why we don't need a new theory and how we move forward from here*, The academy of management perspectives, 24(3), 37-57, 2010.

Dando N., Swift T., *Transparency and assurance minding the credibility gap*, Journal of Business Ethics, 44(2-3), 195-200, 2003.

Danovi A., Quagli A., *Gestione della crisi aziendale e dei processi di risanamento. Prevenzione e diagnosi, terapie, casi aziendali*, Ipsoa, Milano, 2008.

Dart R., *The legitimacy of social enterprise*, Nonprofit management and leadership, 14(4), 411-424, 2004.

De Villiers C., Rinaldi L., Unerman J., *Integrated Reporting: Insights, gaps and an agenda for future research*, Accounting, Auditing and Accountability Journal, 27(7), 1042-1067, 2014.

Deegan C., Newson M., *Environmental performance evaluation and reporting for private and public organisations*, Sydney, Environmental Protection Authority, 1996.

Dees J.G., Emerson J., Economy P., *Enterprising nonprofits: A toolkit for social entrepreneurs*, New York, NY, John and Son, 2001.

Defourny J., Nyssens M., *Conceptions of social enterprise and social entrepreneurship in Europe and the United States: Convergences and divergences*, Journal of social entrepreneurship, 1(1), 32-53, 2010.

Defourny J., Nyssens M., S*ocial enterprise in Europe: recent trends and developments*, Social enterprise journal, 4(3), 202-228, 2008.

Demsetz H., Villalonga B., *Ownership structure and corporate performance*, Journal of corporate finance, 7(3), 209-233, 2001.

Doane D., *Corporate spin: The troubled teenage years of social reporting*, London, New Economics Foundation, 2000.

Dodgson M., Gann D.M., Phillips N., *The Oxford handbook of innovation management*, OUP Oxford, 2014.

Donaldson T., Preston L.E., *The stakeholder theory of the corporation: Concepts, evidence, and implications*, Academy of management Review, 20(1), 65-91, 1995.

Donaldson T., Preston L., *La teoria degli stakeholder dell'impresa: concetti, evidenza ed implicazioni*, in Freeman E.R., Rusconi G., Dorigatti M., *Teoria degli stakeholder*, Franco Angeli, Milano, 2007.

Dossena G., *Risanamento, governance e stakeholder: gestione di interessi in conflitto e conflitto di interessi*, Sinergie rivista di studi e ricerche, 71, 2011.

Drayton W., *The citizen sector: Becoming as entrepreneurial and competitive as business*, California management review, 44(3), 120-132, 2002.

Drucker P.F., *Post-capitalist society*, New York, NY, Harper Business, 1993.

Du S., Bhattacharya C.B., Sen S., *Maximizing business returns to corporate social responsibility (CSR): The role of CSR communication*, International Journal of Management Reviews, 12(1), 8-19, 2010.

Ebrahim A., Battilana J., Mair J., *The governance of social enterprises: Mission drift and accountability challenges in hybrid organizations*, Research in Organizational Behavior, 34, 81-100, 2014.

Ebrahim A., Rangan, V.K., *What impact?. A framework for measuring the scale and scope of social performance*, California Management Review, 56(3), 118-141, 2014.

Emery F., Trist E., *The casual texture of organizational environments*, Human relations, 1966.

Emirbayer M., Goodwin J., *Network analysis, culture, and the problem of agency*, American journal of sociology, 99(6), 1411-1454, 1994.

Epstein M.J., Buhovac A.R., *Making sustainability work: Best practices in managing and measuring corporate social, environmental, and economic impacts*, Berrett-Koehler Publishers, 2014.

Epstein M.J., *Implementing corporate sustainability: Measuring and managing social and environmental impacts*, Strategic Finance, 89(7), 24-31, 2008.

Epstein M.J., *Measuring Corporate Environmental Performance: Best Practices for Costing and Managing an Effective Environmental Strategy*, Irwin, Chicago, IL, 1996.

Epstein M., *Making sustainability work: Best practices in managing and measuring corporate social, environmental, and economic impacts*, Sheffield: Greenleaf, 2008.

European Commission, Directorate General for Employment, *Promoting a European Framework for Corporate Social Responsibility: Green Paper*, Office for Official Publications of the European Communities, DOC 01/9, 18 July, 2001.

European Parliament, *Directive 2014/95/EU*, Council of 22 October 2014.

Evan W.M., Freeman R.E., *A stakeholder theory of the modern corporation: Kantian capitalism*, in Beauchamp T., Bowie N., *Ethical Theory and Business*, Prentice Hall, Englewood Cliffs, 75-93, 1988.

Fahey L., Narayanan V.K., *Macroenvironmental analysis for strategic management*, St. Paul: West, 1986.

Fama E.F., Jensen M.C., *Separation of ownership and control*, The journal of law and Economics, 26(2), 301-325, 1983.

Ferrero G., *Impresa e management*, Giuffrè, Milano, 1987.

Figge F., Hahn T., Schaltegger S., Wagner M., *The sustainability balanced scorecard – linking sustainability management to business strategy*, Business strategy and the Environment, 11(5), 269-284, 2002.

Fink S., *Crisis management: Planning for the inevitable*, American Management Association, 1986.

Freeman R.E., Reed D.L., *Stockholders and stakeholders: A new perspective on corporate governance*, California management review, 25(3), 88-106, 1983.

Freeman R.E., *Strategic Management: A Stakeholder approach, Pitman*, Boston, MA, 1984.

Freeman R.E., *Strategic management: A stakeholder approach*. Cambridge University press, 2010.

Funk K., *Sustainability and performance*, MIT Sloan, Management Review, 44(2), 65, 2003.

Gamerschlag R., Möller K., Verbeeten F., *Determinants of voluntary CSR disclosure: empirical evidence from Germany*, Review of Managerial Science, 5(2-3), 233-262, 2011.

Ganley D., Lampe C., *The ties that bind: Social network principles in online communities*, Decision Support Systems, 47(3), 266-274, 2009.

Gao S.S., Zhang J.J., Stakeholder engagement, social auditing and corporate sustainability, Business process management journal, 12(6), 722-740, 2006.

Garriga E., Melé D., *Corporate social responsibility theories: Mapping the territory*, Journal of business ethics, 53(1), 51-71, 2004.

Garrison R.H., Noreen E.W., Brewer P.C., *Managerial accounting*. New York: McGraw-Hill/Irwin, 2003.

Gawell M., Johannisson B., Lundqvist M., *Entrepreneurship in the name of society*, Stockholm: KK Foundation, 2009.

Gond J.P., Grubnic S., Herzig C., Moon J., *Configuring management control systems: Theorizing the integration of strategy and sustainability*, Management Accounting Research, 23(3), 205-223, 2012.

Graham-Nye J., *B Corporations: A New Kind of Company Needing a New Kind of Funding Model*, in Huffington Post, April 30, 2015, available online at http://www.huffingtonpost.com/jason-grahamnye/B Corporations-a-new-kind_b_7174520.html, accessed on November 28, 2017.

Grant R.M., *Contemporary Strategy Analysis: Concepts, Techniques, Applications*, Oxford, Blackwell Publishers, 2005.

Gray R. H., *Corporate reporting for sustainable development: Accounting for sustainability in 2000AD*, Environmental Values, 17-45, 1994.

Gray R. H., *Current developments and trends in social and environmental auditing, reporting and attestation: A review and comment*, International Journal of Auditing, 4(3), 247-268, 2000.

Gray R.H., *The social accounting project and accounting, organizations and society: Privileging engagement, imagination, new accountings and pragmatism over Critique?*, Accounting, Organizations and Society, 27(7), 687-708, 2002.

Gray R., Owen D.L., Adams C., *Accounting and accountability: Social and environmental accounting in a changing world*, Harlow, England, and New York, Financial Times/Prentice Hall, 1996.

Gray R., Javad M., Power D.M., Sinclair C.D., *Social and environmental disclosure and corporate characteristics: A research note and extension*, Journal of business finance & accounting, 28(3-4), 327-356, 2001.

GRI, *Consolidated set of GRI Sustainability Reporting Standards*, 2016, Retrieved October 15, 2017, from Global Reporting Initiative: https://www.globalreporting.org/standards/.

GRI, U. WBSCDSDG compass, *The guide for business action on the SDGs*, SDG Compass, 2015.

Grunig J.E., White J., *The effect of worldviews on public relations theory and practice*, Excellence in public relations and communication management, 31-64, 1992.

Grunig L.A., Grunig J.E., Ehling W.P., *What is an effective organization*, Excellence in public relations and communication management, 65-90, 1992.

Guthrie J., Petty R., Yongvanich K., Ricceri F., *Using content analysis as a research method to inquire into intellectual capital reporting*, Journal of intellectual capital, 5(2), 282-293, 2004.

Hart S.L., *Capitalism at the crossroads*, Johnson Graduate School of Management, Cornell University, Wharton School Publishing, 2005.

Hartigan P., *It's about people, not profits*, Business Strategy Review, 17(4), 42-45, 2006.

Heil O., Robertson T.S., *Toward a theory of competitive market signaling: A research agenda*, Strategic Management Journal, 12(6), 403-418, 1991.

Heller K., *Return to community*, American Journal of Community Psychology, 17(1), 1-15. 1989.

Henderson D., *Misguided virtue, False notions of corporate social responsibility*, Wellington, 2001.

Henkel M., *Academic identity and autonomy in a changing policy environment*, Higher education, 49(1-2), 155-176, 2005.

Henton D., Melville J., Walesh K., *The age of the civic entrepreneur: restoring civil society and building economic community*, National Civic Review, 86(2), 149-156, 1997.

Heracleous L., *What is the impact of corporate governance on organisational performance?*, Corporate governance: an international review, 9(3), 165-173, 2001.

Hillery G.A., *Definition of community*, Rural sociology, 20, 111-123, 1955.

Hillman A.J., Keim G.D., *Shareholder value, stakeholder management, and social issues: What's the bottom line?*, Strategic management journal, 22(2), 125-139, 2001.

House R.J., et al., *Culture, leadership, and organizations: The GLOBE study of 62 societies*, Sage publications, 2004.

Husted B.W., Allen D.B., *Corporate social strategy in multinational enterprises: Antecedents and value creation*, Journal of Business Ethics, 74(4), 345-361, 2007.

IIRC, *The International <IR> Framework*, 2013, Accessed 30 October 2018 at: http://integratedreporting.org/wp-content/uploads/2013/12/13-12-08-THE-INTERNATIONAL-IR-FRAMEWORK-2-1.pdf.

IIRC, *Toward Integrated Reporting. Communicating Value in the 21st Century*, 2011, Accessed 27 September 2017 at: https://integratedreporting.org/wp-content/uploads/2012/06/Discussion-Paper-Summary1.pdf.

International Accounting Standards Board (IASB), *The conceptual framework for financial reporting 2010*, London: IASB, 2010.

Jacques T., *Embedding issue management as a strategic element of crisis prevention*, Disaster Prevention and Management, 19(4), 2010.

Jean-Louis l., Marthe Nyssens M., *The social enterprise Towards a theoretical socio-economic approach*, in Borzaga C., Defourny J., *The emergence of social enterprise*, Vol. 4, Psychology Press, 2004.

Jensen M.C., Meckling W.H., *Theory of the firm: Managerial behavior, agency costs and ownership structure*, Journal of financial economics, 3(4), 305-360, 1976.

Jones T.M., Wicks A.C., Freeman E.R., *Stakeholder theory: the state of art*, in Bowie N.E., *The Blackwell guide to business ethics*, Blackwell Publisher, 2002.

Kaplan R., Norton D., *The Balanced Scorecard – measures that drive performance*, Harvard Business Review, Jan-Feb, 71-79, 1992.

Kaplan R., Norton D., *The Balanced Scorecard: Translating Strategies into Action*, Harvard Business School Press, Boston, MA, 1996.

Kaplan R., Norton D., *The Strategy-Focused Organization: how Balanced Scorecard Companies Thrive in the New Business Environment*, Harvard Business School Press, Boston, MA, 2001.

Kerlin J.A., *A comparative analysis of the global emergence of social enterprise*, Voluntas: international journal of voluntary and nonprofit organizations, 21(2), 162-179, 2010.

Kerlin J.A., *Social enterprise in the United States and Europe: Understanding and learning from the differences*, Voluntas: International Journal of Voluntary and Nonprofit Organizations, 17(3), 246, 2006.

Kim S., Karlesky M., Myers C., Schifeling T., *Why Companies Are Becoming B Corporations*, Harvard Business Review Digital Articles [serial online], June 17, 2-5, 2016, Available from: Business Source Complete, Ipswich, MA. Accessed December 21, 2017.

Kiriakidou O., Millward L.J., *Corporate identity: external reality or internal fit?*, Corporate Communications: An International Journal, 5(1), 49-58, 2000.

Klöpffer W., *Life-cycle based methods for sustainable product development*, International Journal of Life Cycle Assessment, 8(3), 157-159, 2003.

Kochan T.A., Rubinstein S.A., *Toward a stakeholder theory of the firm: The Saturn partnership*, Organization science, 11(4), 367-386, 2000.

Korosec R.L., Berman E.M., *Municipal support for social entrepreneurship*, Public Administration Review, 66(3), 448-462, 2006.

Kotler P., Lee N., *Best of breed: When it comes to gaining a market edge while supporting a social cause, "corporate social marketing" leads the pack*, Social marketing quarterly, 11(3-4), 91-103, 2005.

KPMG, GRI, UNEP CCGA, *Carrots and Sticks: Global Trends in sustainability reporting regulation and policy*, KPMG Advisory NV, Global Reporting Initiative, Centre for Corporate Governance in Africa, United Nations Environment Programme, 2016.

Krippendorff K., *Content Analysis: An Introduction to its Methodology*, Sage, Beverly Hills, USA, 1980.

Kroeger A., Weber C., *Developing a conceptual framework for comparing social value creation*, Academy of Management Review, 39(4), 513-540, 2014.

Lamberton G., *Sustainability accounting – A brief history and conceptual framework*, Accounting Forum, 29(1), 7-26, 2005.

Larsen B., Häversjö T., *Management by standards – Real benefits from fashion*, Scandinavian Journal of Management, 17(4), 457-480, 2001.

Lawrence T.B., Dover G., Gallagher B., Managing social innovation, in Dodgson M., Gann D.M., Phillips N., *The oxford handbook of innovation management*, OUP Oxford, 316-334, 2014.

Leadbetter C., *The rise of the social entrepreneur*, Demos, London, 1997.

Lehman G., *Disclosing new worlds: A role for social and environmental accounting and auditing*, Accounting, Organizations and Society, 24(3), 217-241, 1999.

Licht A.N., Goldschmidt C., Schwartz S.H., *Culture rules: The foundations of the rule of law and other norms of governance*, Journal of comparative economics, 35(4), 659-688, 2007.

Licht A., *The Maximands of Corporate Governance: A Theory of Values and Cognitive Style*, Delaware Journal of Corporate Law, 29, 649, 2004.

Light P.C., *Reshaping social entrepreneurship*, Stanford Social Innovation Review, 4(3), 47-51, 2006.

Lockett A., Moon J., Visser W., *Corporate social responsibility in management research: Focus, nature, salience and sources of influence*, Journal of management studies, 43(1), 115-136, 2006.

Lubatkin M., Lane P.J., Collin S., Very P., *A nationally-bounded theory of opportunism in corporate governance*, University of Connecticut, 2001.

Lydenberg S.D., Rogers J., Wood D., *From transparency to performance: Industry-based sustainability reporting on key issues*, Cambridge, MA, Hauser Center for Nonprofit Organizations, 2010.

Maas K., Liket K., *Social impact measurement: Classification of methods*, in Burritt R., Schaltegger S., Bennett M., Pohjola T., Csutora M., *Environmental management accounting and supply chain management, eco-efficiency in industry and science*, Vol. 27, Delft, The Netherlands, Springer 2011.

Maccaferri A., *Arriva la carica delle B Corporation che vogliono riscrivere l'economia*, Il Sole 24 Ore, 2016.

MacDonald J.P., *Strategic planning for sustainability using the ISO14001 standard*, Journal of Cleaner Production, 13(6), 631-643, 2005.

Mair J., Martí I., *Social entrepreneurship research: A source of explanation, prediction, and delight*, Journal of World Business, 41(1), 36-44, 2006.

Mair J., Robinson J., Hockerts K., *Social entrepreneurship*, New York, Palgrave Macmillan, 2006.

Mandich G., *Spazio tempo. Prospettive sociologiche*, Franco Angeli, Milano, 1996.

Manetti, G., Becatti L., Assurance services for sustainability reports: Standards and empirical evidence. *Journal of Business Ethics*, 87(1), 289-298, 2009.

Margolis J.D., Walsh J.P., *Misery loves companies: Rethinking social initiatives by business*, Administrative science quarterly, 48(2), 268-305, 2003.

Marquis C., Battilana J., *Acting globally but thinking locally? The enduring influence of local communities on organizations*, Research in organizational behavior, 29, 283-302, 2009.

Marquis C., Glynn M.A., Davis G.F., *Community isomorphism and corporate social action*, Academy of management review, 32(3), 925-945, 2007.

Martin R.L., Osberg S., *Social entrepreneurship: The case for definition*, 5(2), 28-39, Stanford social innovation review, 2007.

Martin R., *The Virtue Matrix: Calculating the Return on Corporate Responsibility*, Harvard Business Review, 80(3), 2002.

Masini C., *Lavoro e risparmio*, Utet, Torino, 1979.

Massetti B.L., *The social entrepreneurship matrix as a "tipping point" for economic change*, Emergence: Complexity and Organization, 10(3), 1, 2008.

Matacena A., Del Baldo M., *Responsabilità sociale d'impresa e territorio. L'esperienza delle piccole e medie imprese marchigiane*, Franco Angeli, Milano, 2009.

Matacena A., *L'accountability nelle imprese sociali*, Non profit, 12(4), 653-674, 2006.

Mathews M.R., *Socially responsible accounting*, London, Chapman & Hall, 1993.

Mathews R., *Developing a matrix approach to categorise the social and environmental accounting research literature*, Qualitative Research in Accounting & Management, 1(1), 30-45, 2004.

Matten D., Moon J., *"Implicit" and "explicit" CSR: A conceptual framework for a comparative understanding of corporate social responsibility*, Academy of management Review, 33(2), 404-424, 2008.

McWilliams A., Siegel D.S., Wright P.M., *Corporate social responsibility: Strategic implications*, Journal of management studies, 43(1), 1-18, 2006.

McWilliams A., Siegel D., *Corporate social responsibility: A theory of the firm perspective*, Academy of management review, 26(1), 117-127, 2001.

Meek G.K., Gray S. J., *The value added statement: an innovation for US companies*, Accounting Horizons, 2(2), 73, 1988.

Michelon G., Parbonetti A., *The effect of corporate governance on sustainability disclosure*, Journal of Management & Governance, 16 (3), 477-509, 2012.

Milne M.J., Adler R.W., *Exploring the reliability of social and environmental disclosures content analysis*, Accounting, Auditing and Accountability Journal, 12(2), 237-256, 1999.

Milne M.J., Gray R., *W (h) ither ecology? The triple bottom line, the global reporting initiative, and corporate sustainability reporting*, Journal of business ethics, 118(1), 13-29, 2013.

Miolo Vitali P., *Problemi ecologici nella gestione delle aziende*, Giuffrè, Milano, 1978.

Mitroff I.I., Anagnos G., *Managing crises before they happen: what every executive needs to know about crisis management*, Public Relations Quarterly, 46(4), 2001.

Moldan B., Billharz S., Matravers R., *Sustainability Indicators: Report of the Project on Indicators of Sustainable Development*, New York: Wiley, 1997.

Mook L., Quarter J., Richmond B.J., *What counts: Social accounting for nonprofits and cooperatives*, London, Sigel Press, 2007.

Mulgan G., *The process of social innovation*, Innovations: technology, governance, globalization, 1(2), 145-162, 2006.

Mulgan G., Tucker S., Ali R., Sanders B., S*ocial innovation: what it is, why it matters and how it can be accelerated*, 2007.

Murray R., Caulier-Grice J., Mulgan G., *The open book of social innovation*, London, The Young Foundation, 2010.

Nelson, R.R., Winter S.G., *An evolutionary theory of economic change*, Harvard University Press, 2009.

Nicholls A., *The legitimacy of social entrepreneurship: reflexive isomorphism in a pre-paradigmatic field*, Entrepreneurship theory and practice, 34(4), 611-633, 2010.

Nicholls A., *We do good things don't we? Blended value accounting in social entrepreneurship*, Accounting, Organizations and Society, 34 (6-7): 755-69, 2009.

Nicholls J., Lawlor E., Neitzert E., Goodspeed T., *A guide to social return on investment*, Lothian, The SROI Network, 2012.

Nicholls J., Lawlor E., Neitzert E., Goodspeed T., *A guide to social return on investment*, London, Office of the Third Sector, Cabinet Office, 2009.

Nicholls J., *Measuring Social Impact*, Pioneers Post Quarterly, Summer, 1, 49-53, 2015.

Nicholls, A., Cho A., *Social Enterpreneurship: The Structuration of a Field*, in Nicholls A., *Social Entrepreneurship: New Models of Sustainable Social Change*, 99-118, 2006.

Nyssens M., *Social Enterprise – At the Crossroads of Market, Public Policies and Civil Society*, Routledge, New York, 2006.

OECD, *Corporate social responsibility: Partners for progress*, Paris, OECD, 2001.

Orij R., *Corporate social disclosures in the context of national cultures and stakeholder theory*, Accounting, Auditing and Accountability Journal, 23(7), 868-889, 2010.

Parkinson J., Gamble A., Kelly G., *The political economy of the company*, Oxford, Hart Publishing, 2001.

Paton R., *Managing and measuring social enterprises*, Sage Publications, London, 2003.

Patrick D.L., Wickizer T.M., *Community and health*, in Amick B.C., Levine S., Tarlov A.R., Walsh D.C., *Society and Health*, New York, NY, Oxford University Press Inc, 46-92, 1995.

Pava M.L., Krausz J., *The association between corporate social-responsibility and financial performance: The paradox of social cost*, Journal of business Ethics, 15(3), 321-357, 1996.

Pearson C.M., Clair J.A., *Reframing crisis management*, Academy of management review, 23(1), 59-76, 1998.

Pearson C.M., Mitroff I.I., *From crisis prone to crisis prepared: A framework for crisis management*, The academy of management executive, 7(1), 48-59, 1993.

Perez E.A., Correa Ruiz C., Carrasco Fenech F., *Environmental management systems as an embedding mechanism: a research note*, Accounting, Auditing and Accountability Journal 20(3), 403-422, 2007.

Perrini F., *SMEs and CSR theory: Evidence and implications from an Italian perspective*, Journal of business ethics, 67(3), 305-316, 2006.
Perrini F., Tencati A., *Sustainability and stakeholder management: the need for new corporate performance evaluation and reporting systems*, Business Strategy and the Environment, 15(5), 296-308, 2006.
Pfeffer J., Salancik G., *The external control of organization*, Harper, New York, 1978.
Phills J.A., Deigleimer K., Miller D.T., *Rediscovering Social Innovation*, Stanford Social Innovation Review, 6(4), 34-43, 2008.
Poksinska B., Jörn Dahlgaard J., Eklund J.A., *Implementing ISO 14000 in Sweden: motives, benefits and comparisons with ISO 9000*, International Journal of Quality and Reliability Management, 20(5), 585-606, 2003.
Pollach I., Scharl A., Weichselbraun A., *Web content mining for comparing corporate and third-party online reporting: a case study on solid waste management*, Business strategy and the environment, 18(3), 137-148, 2009.
Porter M.E., *Il vantaggio competitivo*, Edizioni di comunità, Milano, 1987.
Porter M.E., Kramer M.R., *Creating shared value*, Harvard Business Review, 89 (1/2), 62-77, 2011.
Porter M.E., Kramer M.R., *Strategy and society: the link between corporate social responsibility and competitive advantage*, Harvard business review, 84(12), 78-92, 2006.
Power M., *Making things auditable*, Accounting, organizations and society, 21(2-3), 289-315, 1996.

Ranalli F., *Il sistema aziendale: aspetti costitutivi ed evolutivi*, in Cavalieri E., Ranalli F., *Economia Aziendale vol. II. Aree funzionali e governo aziendale*, Giappichelli, Torino, 1999.
Rasche A., Esser D.E., *From stakeholder management to stakeholder accountability*, Journal of business ethics, 65(3), 251-267, 2006.
Rattalma M.F., *The Dieselgate: A Legal Perspective*, Springer, 2017.
Razek J., Hosch G., Ives M., *Introduction to governmental and not-for-profit organizations*, Englewood Cliffs, NJ, Prentice Hall, 2000.
Reinhardt C.S., *Evaluating methods for estimating program effects*, The American Journal of Evaluation, 32(2), 246-272, 2011.
Reverte C., *Determinants of corporate social responsibility disclosure ratings by Spanish listed firms*, Journal of Business Ethics, 88(2), 351-366, 2009.
Riahi-Belkaoui A., *Value added reporting and research: state of the art*, Greenwood Publishing Group, 1999.
Robert K-H., *Tools and concepts for sustainable development, how do they relate to a general framework for sustainable development, and to each other?*, Journal of Cleaner Production, 8(3), 243-254, 2000.
Robert K-H., Schmidt-Bleek B., Aloiside Larderel J., Basile G., Jansen L., Kuehr R., et al. *Strategic sustainable developmentd selection, design and synergies of applied tools.* Journal of Cleaner Production, 10(3), 197-214, 2002.
Roberts S., *Supply chain specific? Understanding the patchy success of ethical sourcing initiatives*, Journal of Business Ethics, 44(2-3), 159-170, 2003.
Rowley T.I., Moldoveanu M., *When will stakeholder groups act? An interest-and*

identity-based model of stakeholder group mobilization, Academy of management review, 28(2), 204-219, 2003.

Santos F.M., *A positive theory of social entrepreneurship*, Journal of business ethics, 111(3), 335-351, 2012.

Schaltegger S., Bennett M., Burritt R., *Sustainability accounting and reporting*, Vol. 21, Springer Science & Business Media, 2006.

Schaltegger S., Burritt R.L., *Sustainability accounting for companies: Catchphrase or decision support for business leaders?*, Journal of World Business, 45(4), 375-384, 2010.

Schaltegger S., Burritt R., Petersen H., *An introduction to corporate environmental management: Striving for sustainability*, Routledge, 2017.

Schaltegger S., Figge F., *Environmental shareholder value: economic success with corporate environmental management*, Corporate Social-Responsibility and Environmental Management, 7(1), 29, 2000.

Schaltegger S., Wagner M., *Integrative management of sustainability performance, measurement and reporting*, International Journal of Accounting, Auditing and Performance Evaluation, 3(1), 1-19, 2006.

Schein E.H., *Organizational culture and leadership*, Vol. 356, John Wiley & Sons, 2006.

Scherer A.G., Palazzo G., *The new political role of business in a globalized world: A review of a new perspective on CSR and its implications for the firm, governance, and democracy*, Journal of management studies, 48(4), 899-931, 2011.

SEC, *Climate Change Guidance*, 8/02/2010.

SEC, *Concept Release*, 81 Fed. Reg. 23916, 22/04/2016.

Seeger M.W., Sellnow T.L., Ulmer R.R., *Communication, organization, and crisis*, Annals of the International Communication Association, 21(1), 231-276, 1998.

Seelos C., Mair J., Battilana J., Dacin T.M., *The embeddedness of social entrepreneurship: Understanding variation across local communities*, in *Communities and organizations*, Emerald Group Publishing Limited, 2011.

Seelos C., Mair J., *Innovation is not the Holy Grail*, Stanford Social Innovation Review, 10(4), 44-49, 2012.

Seelos C., Mair J., *Innovation and scaling for impact: How effective social enterprises do it*, Stanford University Press, 2017.

Segarra M.B., Prepared Cfo [serial online], April 2014, 30(3), 42-45, Available from: Business Source Complete, Ipswich, MA. Accessed December 21, 2017.

Sellnow T.L., *Scientific argument in organizational crisis communication: The case of Exxon*, Argumentation and Advocacy, 30(1), 28-42, 1993.

Short J.C., Moss T.W., Lumpkin G.T., *Research in social entrepreneurship: Past contributions and future opportunities*, Strategic entrepreneurship journal, 3(2), 161-194, 2009.

Simmel G., Frisby D., *M. Featherstone, Simmel on Culture: Selected Writings*, Sage Publications Inc., 1997.

Social Enterprise U.K., *The people's business: state of social enterprise survey 2013*, London, Social Enterprise UK, 2013.

Somers A.B., *Shaping the balanced scorecard for use in UK social enterprises*, Social Enterprise Journal, 1(1), 43-56, 2005.

Sorge A., *The global and the local: Understanding the dialectics of business systems*, Oxford, Oxford University Press, 2005.

Stephens K.K., Malone P., *New media for crisis communication: Opportunities for technical translation, dialogue, and stakeholder responses*, in Coombs W.T., Holladay S.J., *The handbook of crisis communication*, 381-395, 2010.

Stewart J.D., *The role of information in public accountability*, Issues in public sector accounting, 17, 13-34, 1984.

Stiglitz J.E., *Capital market liberalization, economic growth, and instability*, World development, 28(6), 1075-1086, 2000.

Stuart T.E., Sorenson O., *Strategic networks and entrepreneurial ventures*, Strategic Entrepreneurship Journal, 1(3-4), 211-227, 2007.

Sullivan Mort G., Weerawardena, J. Carnegie K., *Social entrepreneurship: Towards conceptualisation*, International journal of nonprofit and voluntary sector marketing, 8(1), 76-88, 2003.

Suojanen W.W., *Accounting theory and the large corporation*, Accounting Review, 391-398, 1954.

Swanson L.A., Di Zhang D., *The social entrepreneurship zone*, Journal of Nonprofit and Public Sector Marketing, 22(2), 71-88, 2010.

Tencati A., *Sostenibilità, impresa e performance. Un nuovo modello di evaluation and reporting*, Egea, Milano, 2002.

Thake S., Zadek S., *Practical People, Noble Causes: How to Support Community-based Social Entrepreneurs. Executive Summary*, New Economics Foundation, 1997.

The SROI Network, *A guide to social return on investment, Liverpool*, UK: SROI, 2012.

Thompson J.L., *Social enterprise and social entrepreneurship: where have we reached? A summary of issues and discussion points*, Social Enterprise Journal, 4(2), 149-161, 2008.

Tönnies F., Harris J., *Community and civil society*, Vol. 266, Cambridge, Cambridge University, 2001.

Toppinen A., Li N., Tuppura A., Xiong Y., *Corporate responsibility and strategic groups in the forest-based industry: Exploratory analysis based on the Global Reporting Initiative (GRI) framework*, Corporate Social Responsibility and Environmental Management, 19(4), 191-205, 2012.

Tsui A.S., Nifadkar S.S., Ou A.Y., *Cross-national, cross-cultural organizational behavior research: Advances, gaps, and recommendations*, Journal of management, 33(3), 426-478, 2007.

Unerman J., Bennett M., *Increased stakeholder dialogue and the Internet: Towards greater corporate accountability or reinforcing capitalist hegemony?*, Accounting, Organizations and Society, 29(7), 685-707, 2004.

Van Staden C.J., Vorster Q., *The usefulness of the value added statement: a review of the literature*, Meditari Accountancy Research, 6, 337-351, 1998.

Waldman D.A., De Luque M.S., Washburn N., House R.J., Adetoun B., Barrasa A., Dorfman P., *Cultural and leadership predictors of corporate social responsibil-

ity values of top management: A GLOBE study of 15 countries, Journal of International Business Studies, 37(6), 823-837, 2006.

Waldman D.A., Siegel D.S., Javidan M., *Components of CEO transformational leadership and corporate social responsibility*, Journal of management studies, 43(8), 1703-1725, 2006.

Watzlawick P., Weakland J.H., Fisch R., *Change: Principles of problem formation and problem resolution*, WW Norton & Company, 2011.

Weber M., T*he business case for corporate social responsibility: A company-level measurement approach for CSR*, European Management Journal, 26(4), 247-261, 2008.

Weerawardena J., Mort G.S., *Investigating social entrepreneurship: A multidimensional model*, Journal of world business, 41(1), 21-35, 2006.

Weick K., *Enacted sensemaking in crisis situation*, Journal of Management Studies, 25(4), 1998.

Westley F., Antadze N., *Making a difference: Strategies for scaling social innovation for greater impact*, Innovation Journal, 15(2), 2010, article 2, Accessed online 26, november 2017 at: https://www.innovation.cc/scholarly-style/westley2antadze2make_difference_final.pdf.

White H., *A contribution to current debates in impact evaluation*, Evaluation, 16(2), 153-164, 2010.

Williamson O.E., *Organization form, residual claimants, and corporate control*, The Journal of Law and Economics, 26(2), 351-366, 1983.

Willis C.L., *Definitions of community, II: an examination of definitions of community since 1950*, South Sociologist, 9, 14-19, 1977.

Wood D.J., *Corporate social performance revisited*, Academy of management review, 16(4), 691-718, 1991.

Wright S., Nelson J.D., Cooper J.M., Murphy S., *An evaluation of the transport to employment (T2E) scheme in Highland Scotland using social return on investment (SROI)*, Journal of Transport Geography, 17(6), 457-467, 2009.

Wry T., York J.G., *An identity-based approach to social enterprise*, Academy of Management Review, 42(3), 437-460, 2017.

Xu K., Li W., *An ethical stakeholder approach to crisis communication: A case study of Foxconn's 2010 employee suicide crisis*, Journal of Business Ethics, 117(2), 371-386, 2013.

Yunus M., *Building social business: The new kind of capitalism that serves humanity's most pressing needs*, Public Affairs, 2011.

Zahra S.A., Gedajlovic E., Neubaum D.O., Shulman J.M., *A typology of social entrepreneurs: Motives, search processes and ethical challenges*, Journal of business venturing, 24(5), 519-532, 2009.

Zavani M., *Il valore della comunicazione aziendale. Rilevanza e caratteri dell'informativa sociale e ambientale*, Torino, Giappichelli, 2000.

For Product Safety Concerns and Information please contact our EU
representative GPSR@taylorandfrancis.com
Taylor & Francis Verlag GmbH, Kaufingerstraße 24, 80331 München, Germany

www.ingramcontent.com/pod-product-compliance
Ingram Content Group UK Ltd.
Pitfield, Milton Keynes, MK11 3LW, UK
UKHW020949180425
457613UK00019B/609